MW00808927

Breakfast with Barth

Breakfast with Barth

DAILY DEVOTIONS

Donald K. McKim

CASCADE *Books* · Eugene, Oregon

BREAKFAST WITH BARTH
Daily Devotions

Cascade Books
An Imprint of Wipf and Stock Publishers
199 W. 8th Ave., Suite 3
Eugene, OR 97401

www.wipfandstock.com

PAPERBACK ISBN: 978-1-5326-5094-9
HARDCOVER ISBN: 978-1-5326-5095-6
EBOOK ISBN: 978-1-5326-5096-3

Cataloguing-in-Publication data:

Names: McKim, Donald K., author. | Barth, Karl, author.

Title: Breakfast with Barth : Daily Devotions / Donald McKim.

Description: Eugene, OR : Cascade Books, 2019 | Includes index.

Identifiers: ISBN 978-1-5326-5094-9 (paperback) | ISBN 978-1-5326-5095-6 (hardcover) | ISBN 978-1-5326-5096-3 (ebook)

Subjects: LCSH: Barth, Karl,—1886–1968. | Spiritual life. | Religious life. | Theology, Doctrinal. | Pastoral theology.

Classification: LCC BX4827.B3 M35 2019 (print) | LCC BX4827.B3 (ebook)

Manufactured in the U.S.A.

For Robert Benedetto and Clifford Anderson
Wonderful friends, esteemed scholars, and faithful witnesses to Jesus Christ
With gratitude

Contents

Preface

I have had a long-standing interest in Karl Barth (1886–1968). Barth was the major Protestant theologian of the twentieth century. He wrote more theology than anyone since Thomas Aquinas (1225–74). Barth's thirteen-volume *Church Dogmatics* is a magnificent combination of theological discussion engaged with biblical interpretation and in dialogue with the historic doctrines of the Christian church. While all Barth's perspectives may not be agreed with, they cannot be ignored.

Throughout college, seminary, and my doctoral work, I read Barth and came to see his contributions to the whole of Christian theology. A strong impetus in this direction were the seminary professors who became interpreters of Barth to me.

When I was a student at Pittsburgh Theological Seminary (1971–74), Karl Barth's son, Markus Barth, was a Professor of New Testament. Markus Barth's presence and his classes brought emphases of his father's theology, but also gave a close-up look at how a biblical scholar interpreted biblical texts, interpretations that for Markus Barth were often closely congruent with his father's views. Barth's major, two-volume commentary on Ephesians was written during his Pittsburgh years. Markus's earlier interpretations, especially on baptism, were influential for his father's views.

Later, when I taught theology at the University of Dubuque Theological Seminary during the 1980s, Markus Barth gave lectures at the seminary. This seminary had been his first American teaching position. Then, Markus met our young son, Karl, who is named for his father.

The second professor of great importance to me at Pittsburgh Seminary was my theology professor, Arthur C. Cochrane. Arthur Cochrane was a recognized authority of Barth's theology having studied with Barth in the early 1930s. Through courses on Barth with Dr. Cochrane and personal friendship, Barth became an important theological figure for me. Some Pittsburgh Seminary students and I attended the inaugural meeting of the Karl Barth Society of North America in Toronto, Canada during those years.

It was to Arthur Cochrane that I dedicated the book I edited in 1986 for the 100th anniversary of Karl Barth's birth, *How Karl Barth Changed My Mind.*[1] This is one of my favorite books I've produced. I solicited essays from twenty-six contemporary theologians on the title's theme, a play on the long-standing series in *The Christian Century*: "How My Mind Has Changed." The book provides a freeze-frame of contemporary theology a century after Barth's birth, as well as tracing trajectories of influence from Barth to leading theologians of the day. My dedication of this book was: "To Arthur C. Cochrane. Reformed theologian, churchman, and scholar of Karl Barth with whom I first studied Barth and whose life has been a faithful witness to 'the Word made flesh.' With gratitude and appreciation."

Through years of seminary teaching, being a pastor, and an editor for Presbyterian Publishing Corporation, Barth has always been "present" through my reading, writing, teaching, and reflections. I never forget Karl Barth's desk. It was his father's desk and on it Barth wrote his *Church Dogmatics*. The desk was given to Pittsburgh Theological Seminary in exchange for a new desk for Barth. Barth felt he got the better end of the deal! Barth's desk is now found in Barbour Library at Pittsburgh Seminary and used to be in the library's foyer, next to the card catalogue (when such resources existed!). During my years as a seminary and a doctoral student, I would see Barth's desk on an almost daily basis, especially as I worked on my doctoral dissertation in the carrel, one floor

1. McKim, *How Karl Barth Changed My Mind.*

below. It was a constant impetus for me to engage in theological study, represented by Barth's desk.[2]

Karl Barth was a preeminent church theologian, so it is appropriate that his desk is housed in a theological seminary library. His theology, while technical in a theological sense, is also a theology for the church, for Christian people who seek to be a witness to God's love in Jesus Christ, by the power of the Holy Spirit. As one who hopes to be a church theologian myself, I have been particularly motivated in the past several years to try to present insights from important theologians in a form that will be accessible and of interest to laypersons and those who have not engaged in formal theological study.

Recognizing that most of these persons will not be turning to the primary works of the great theologians, I have tried to provide books that introduce their theological thought in the form of citing a quotation from their writings and then writing a one-page devotion on the quote. The purpose is to explain the meaning of the quotation in the theologian's overall theology, and to raise reflections about what that theological insight can mean for the church and for Christian living today. My hope is that in bite-sized bits, in the form of a devotion that might be read daily or occasionally, those without formal theological training will be able to get insights and a flavor of the theologies of important theologians.

I have used this approach for John Calvin, Martin Luther, Dietrich Bonhoeffer, and now, Karl Barth.[3] *Breakfast with Barth: Daily Devotions* conveys insights from Barth's writings into devotional pieces to stimulate theological thinking, and reflections on what Barth's insights can mean for living a Christian life in the context of the church. I always say the question is the one from the book of Ezekiel: "Can these bones live?" (Ezek 37:3). Can the theology of the great theologians be understood and appropriated

2. For the story of Barth's desk and chair coming to Pittsburgh Seminary, see McKim, *Ever a Vision*, 42. See the photo of Barth's desk and the devotion, "A Prodigious Index Finger" below.

3. See McKim, *Coffee with Calvin*; McKim, *Moments with Martin Luther*; McKim, *Mornings with Bonhoeffer*.

by today's Christians to deepen our understandings and help us in living our Christian lives as we serve Jesus Christ? I hope this book can serve these purposes.

The two parts of the book, "Believing as a Christian" and "Living as a Christian," divide the devotions. But all have the same purposes. The devotions are in no specific order, but I have tried to move progressively through general themes. They do not try to provide a full overview of Barth's theology, but they do focus on important elements.

The book can be for daily use and the devotions read in order. Or, it can be dipped into occasionally with no apparent order to the readings. In either case, the hope is—theologically!—that the Holy Spirit will use the devotions to bless the lives of those who read, no matter what devotion is read or when it is read.

My thanks for help with this book go to Robin Parry of Wipf & Stock Publishers who has been enthusiastic and supportive of this project. I am most grateful to him, as always. The fine folks at Wipf & Stock have been excellent colleagues in the production of this volume and I am most appreciative to them. They carry out important ministries.

My wonderful family provides love and care which enables writing. I can never express the fullness and depth of my love and gratitude to them. LindaJo is my loving wife, whose sustaining support gives joy and purpose to all I do. I thank her more that I can express. Our son, Stephen, and his wife, Caroline, bless us along with their children, Maddie, Annie, and Jack. Our times together are precious. Our son, Karl, and his wife, Lauren, delight us fully and we share happy times together. We are thankful to "the good God" (as Barth would say) for the blessings of life, family, and love in life together.

This book is dedicated to two friends.

Robert Benedetto is a friend from days together at Pittsburgh Seminary. Bob has had a distinguished career in theological librarianship, carefully preserving theological resources and also overseeing important theological libraries. Delightfully, we are coauthors of the *Historical Dictionary of Reformed Churches* for three separate editions. It has been a joy to collaborate, and I am grateful for our friendship and Bob's significant work through the years.

Clifford Anderson is a Barth expert who has led the Center for Barth Studies at Princeton Theological Seminary and contributed to Barth studies in many ways. He has been a fine friend through the years and we enjoy stimulating conversations. Clifford has used his great gifts to benefit theological education and Barth scholarship in meaningful ways. Clifford, Rosanna, and their son, Theodore, bring joy to all.

I hope this book will bring Barth's thought to life in meaningful ways. For those not familiar with Barth, I hope the book will introduce you to "a joyful partisan of the good God."[4] For veteran Barth readers, I hope the book will even deepen your appreciation for Barth's insights.

From Barth we can learn many things. Among them is that "above all," we are "free to rejoice!"[5]

Donald K. McKim
Germantown, Tennessee
August 2018

4. This was the title of an article at Christmas, 1959, on Barth in the German news magazine, *Der Spiegel*.

5. Barth, *Church Dogmatics*, IV/3/1, 247.

Using This Book

This is a book of devotions or reflections on quotations from the Swiss theologian Karl Barth (1886–1968). Each piece is meant to explain the meaning of the Barth quotation and to reflect on the theological meaning of the quotation for the church and for Christian life today. The quotes are drawn from a range of Barth's many writings. Quotations in the devotion without a footnote are drawn from the same page as the Barth quotation at the top of each devotion.

This book can be used by both groups and individuals. The selections are appropriate for use in various church gatherings. Individuals can use the pieces during times of reflection and devotion.

The book has two parts: "Believing as a Christian" and "Living as a Christian." The selections in each part can be used in the order they appear, or randomly.

Several elements can be helpful in using the book:

Read the devotion. Each piece is written compactly, so each sentence is important. The individual sentences can be a source for reflection as each are read. After each sentence, pause and reflect on its meaning.

Meditate on the quotation and devotion. Questions relating to Barth's quotation and the devotion that follow can help focus meditation:

- What is Barth saying here?

- What does Barth's thought mean for the life of the church?
- What does Barth's thought mean for my own life of faith?
- What new or changed attitudes am I led toward through Barth's thought?
- What are ways Barth's thought can be enacted in the life of the church community and in my own life?

Pray about this devotion. Reflect on your meditations and gather your thoughts into a prayer in which you ask God's Holy Spirit to lead you into ways God wants you to believe and live.

Act on the insights you receive. Decide on ways this devotion can affect your life and begin to put these ways of believing and living into your service for Christ. Reorient ways of living. Follow new directions for your Christian witness according to God's will.

++++

The title of each devotion can be a phrase to bring its key insights to mind. As you review the titles of each devotion, recall the important meanings that emerge from each piece.

If you keep a journal, you can summarize what the quotation/reflection means to you and how it can impact your life. You can periodically review these summaries in the future.

You can also consult titles from the "Selected Resources for Further Reflection" section to read more of Barth's works and works about Karl Barth.

Karl Barth Time Line

(1886–1968)

1886, May 10	Born in Basel
1904	University of Bern
1906	University of Berlin
1907	University of Tübingen
1908	University of Marburg
1908	Ordained in the Swiss Reformed Church
1909	Assistant Pastor in Geneva
1911–21	Pastor in Safenwil
1919	First edition of *Romans*
1921–30	Professor of Theology in Göttingen and Münster
1922	Second edition of *Romans* (Eng. 1935)
1930–35	Professor in Bonn
1932	*Church Dogmatics* I/1 (Eng. 1936; 2nd ed. 1975)
1935–62	Professor in Basel
1939–67	*Church Dogmatics* I/2—IV/4 (Eng. 1956–69)
1962–68	Retirement
1968, December 10	Death in Basel

Karl Barth's Desk

Desk at which Karl Barth wrote his *Church Dogmatics*. Painting by Matthias Grünewald which hung over Barth's desk. On display at Pittsburgh Theological Seminary, Pittsburgh, Pennsylvania. Photo by Donald K. McKim.

Karl Barth's Life

Karl Barth (1886–1968) was born in Basel, Switzerland on May 10, 1886. His father, Fritz Barth, was a minister of the Swiss Reformed Church and a lecturer at the Evangelical School of Preachers in Basel. The Barth family moved to Bern when Fritz Barth became a professor of New Testament.[1]

Barth attended several universities. His theological education at the University of Berlin was marked by his studies with the great liberal theologian Adolf von Harnack (1851–1930). Harnack lectured on the history of Christian dogma (doctrine). Barth also studied the "father" of liberal theology, Friedrich Schleiermacher (1768–1834). Later he was to study under Wilhelm Hermann (1846–1922) and others, so he thoroughly imbibed the teaching of these liberal theologians who taught that the Bible was a human book, the record of the religious experience of ancient people. Theological creeds were unnecessary. In famous lectures, Harnack taught that the essence of Christianity was "the brotherhood of man and the fatherhood of God."[2]

After Barth was ordained, he became pastor of the Reformed Church in Safenwil, a village in North Central Switzerland. His early sermons there emphasized "life" and "experience"—emphases he had learned from his teachers.[3]

But in August 1914, World War I broke out. The newspaper published a statement by ninety-three German intellectuals supporting the war policy of Kaiser William II. To Barth's horror, he

1. The great biography of Barth is Busch, *Karl Barth*.

2. See Harnack, *What Is Christianity?*

3. On Barth's preaching in this period, see Barth and Willimon, *Early Preaching of Karl Barth*. For Barth's preaching during World War I, see Barth, *Unique Time of God*.

found the names of nearly all his theological teachers as supporters of this policy. If this was where their theology and ethics led—to the war policy—Barth decided he could no longer believe their teachings, including their interpretations of the Bible and history. This ended Barth's commitment to the theology of the nineteenth century.

Along with his friend, pastor Eduard Thurneysen, Barth began his own intensive studies. He had long discussions with Christoph Blumhardt (1805–80), who was influenced by German pietism and whose son helped form the Swiss religious-socialist movement. Barth joined the Social Democratic Party in 1915, and sided with Safenwil workers of his congregation in a strike over a just wage. He became known as "the Red Pastor" since the Social Democrats were considered by many as Communists.

Blumhardt stressed the kingdom of God and waiting for God's action while performing whatever God called Christians to do. This came down to one word for Barth: hope.

Barth and Thurneysen turned to the Bible, beginning to read the Old and New Testaments with new eyes. They began to see the Bible as the place where God and God's grace is discovered and unfolds. The Bible does not tell us how to speak about God as much as telling us what God says to us. It does not show us how to find God, but proclaims that God has already found us—in sending God's eternal Son, Jesus Christ, into the world. Christ, the "Word of God" (John 1:1), is found through the witness of the biblical texts, which tell us *who* Jesus Christ is ("the Word made flesh," John 1:14) and *what* Christ has done (died to reconcile the world to God through the forgiveness of sins; Romans 5:8).[4]

Barth wrote a famous commentary on Paul's letter to the Romans (1919), and a second edition (1922) where he practiced theological exegesis. He sought the theological message of the Scriptures, instead of practicing the historical-critical methods of interpretation advocated by his teachers. Behind his biblical

4. For Barth's views of the nature of Scripture, see Rogers and McKim, *Authority and Interpretation of the Bible*, 406–26.

interpretation was Barth's commitment to the church's confession that Jesus Christ is Lord.

In the second edition of *Romans*, Barth developed what came to be known as dialectical theology. Barth and his colleagues sought the inner meaning of Scripture. Basic was recognition of the absolute contrast between God and humanity. Barth stressed the discontinuity between God and humanity. God is God, and we are not God! God is wholly other, over and beyond us as human beings, who are created by God. We, as finite humans, encounter and are confronted by the God who is infinite and eternal. God is wholly other than us.

How then is God known? The New Testament proclaims that God has been revealed in God's eternal Son, who has become a human being: Jesus Christ. This produces the world's great crisis. All history and humanity has been brought under God's judgment by God's becoming a person in Jesus Christ. Humans are confronted by God! In Jesus Christ are God's mercy and judgment. This is the dialectic. All the pride, self-sufficiency, and efforts of humanity fall short of establishing a relationship with God. In the cross of Jesus Christ, God speaks a "No" to all human efforts and claims for themselves. Humans have no security in themselves.

But in God's "No" in the cross of Christ, humans can also hear God's "Yes" in Jesus Christ. God's love sent Christ into the world to die so human sin can be forgiven and God and humanity can be reconciled in a relationship of love and trust. Faith is the means by which humans recognize and trust Christ as God's Son who died for them. God provides righteousness for the world in Jesus Christ. When humans encounter the Word of God, Jesus Christ, and believe in him, reconciliation and salvation become real for them.

This is an astounding message! Barth likened his discovery of the message in Romans of what God has done in Christ to be like a person who tripped in a dark church tower and accidentally reached out and caught a bell-rope to regain balance. Then, the bell sounded out, alarming the whole countryside!

One person said Barth's *Romans* "fell like a bomb on the playground of the theologians."[5] Barth had recovered the essential message of Paul and the whole New Testament. God cannot be discovered by humanity; God can only be revealed. Humans can merely witness to this revelation. Jesus Christ is God's Word, who brought time and eternity together so all humanity could be reconciled to God. Barth said about Romans 3:21 that God in Jesus Christ "pronounces us, His [i.e., God's] enemies, to be His friends."[6] This is the reconciliation of the world as the expression of God's love for the world.

Barth's theology of the Word developed when he was a professor at Göttingen, Münster, Bonn, and then for many years in Basel. Barth's theological project turned into the thirteen-volume *Church Dogmatics*. He had initially begun the project with a volume on *Christian Dogmatics*, but he realized that volume had too many ties to existential philosophy and he now wanted to build dogmatics—or theology—on the basis of Christian doctrine that focuses on the doctrine of Jesus Christ. So Barth began again at the beginning, to rethink all theology as a theology of the grace of God in Jesus Christ.

Barth's *Church Dogmatics* had four main parts:

Word of God	Volume 1
God	Volume 2
Creation	Volume 3
Reconciliation	Volume 4

A fifth volume on redemption was contemplated by Barth, but never written.[7] All the topics are interrelated, and Christol-

5. This comment by the Roman Catholic theologian, Karl Adam, was written in the June 1926 issue of the Roman Catholic monthly *Hochland*. It was quoted by an early interpreter of Barth, John McConnachie, in "Teaching of Karl Barth," 385–86.

6. Barth, *Epistle to the Romans*, 93.

7. Among expositions of the *Church Dogmatics* are McKim and Keller, "Dialogue on the Theology," 19–65, and Bromiley, *Introduction to the Theology*. Other treatments of Barth's theology deal with the *Church Dogmatics* as the main expressions of Barth's thought. A fine introduction to Barth is Franke, *Barth for Armchair Theologians*. An excellent reference work is Burnett,

ogy—the doctrine of Jesus Christ—is certainly central. As Barth said in later lectures: "The object of theology is, in fact, Jesus Christ."[8]

The following devotions draw on *Church Dogmatics*, as well as a number of other Barth writings.

Westminster Handbook to Karl Barth.

8. Barth, *Evangelical Theology*, 189.

BELIEVING AS A CHRISTIAN

1

No Other Book

> There is no other book which witnesses to Jesus Christ apart from Holy Scripture.[1]

++++

Once Karl Barth was asked what was the greatest thing he ever learned. He replied the greatest thing he ever learned was what he learned at his mother's knee: "Jesus loves me, this I know, for the Bible tells me so."[2]

This favorite children's hymn expresses an emphasis of Barth's theology throughout his life. We know of Jesus Christ *from the Bible*. Barth was a strong opponent of natural theology—that we can know of God from the book of nature, by using our powers of reason. He also opposed the view of the liberal theology of his time that we can know of God through human experience, what we understand from our lives. Instead, Barth firmly believed and taught that "there is no other book which witnesses to Jesus Christ apart from Holy Scripture."

For Barth, Jesus Christ is seen to be the focus of the whole Bible. All Scripture witnesses to Jesus Christ. Jesus Christ is the one truth of God's self-revelation. In Jesus Christ, God has become a human person. The Scriptures proclaim that God's word has become flesh in Jesus Christ (John 1:14). The Bible is a unique book because the Scriptures witness to Jesus Christ.

We sometimes take the Scriptures for granted. We treat the Bible with reverence and respect. But do we turn to the Scriptures,

1. Barth, *Church Dogmatics* IV/1, 368.

2. This is a well-known story about Karl Barth. See Barth, *Fragments Grave and Gay*, 124. Martin Rumscheidt mentioned this in his address at the Memorial Service of the University of Toronto for Karl Barth on December 19, 1968. Cf. Olson, "Did Karl Barth Really Say?"

expecting to find there what we will find in no other place: words that point us to the Word of God: Jesus Christ himself? No other book—or source—gives us this knowledge of God in Christ Jesus. Let us turn to the Scriptures expectantly: and learn of Jesus Christ!

2

What God Says to Us

> The Bible does not tell us how we are supposed to talk with God, but rather what God says to us.[3]

++++

On February 6, 1917, Karl Barth gave what became a famous lecture in the church at Leutwil, Germany. It was titled: "The New World in the Bible."

As Barth's theology was developing, his emphasis on the centrality of Holy Scripture as a witness to God's one revelation in Jesus Christ became stronger. Barth stressed that to read the Bible is to enter into a strange, new world. The new world of the Bible is the world of God. We read the Bible as the history of God's relationships with human beings. We read the Scriptures in faith. The Scriptures confute our normal, human understandings of history. The Bible is not about human actions; it's about God's actions. The Bible tells us not about our own abilities to live in this world; but of the growth of God's new world, where God reigns. Will we submit to God's reign, or not?

To put it clearly, the Bible does not present what the right human thoughts about God are. The Bible shows the right thoughts of God about humans. This means "the Bible does not tell us how we are supposed to talk with God, but rather what God says to us." This is the new world the Bible shows us. The Bible does not tell us how to place ourselves in a right relationship with God. Rather, it shows us God's reaching out to humanity through covenants, beginning with the covenant with Abraham in faith (Gen 15:1–6) and finally sealed in Jesus Christ (1 Cor 11:23–26).

Will we enter into the new world of the Bible? Will we say, "I believe?" (Mark 9:24).

3. Barth, *Word of God and Theology*, 25.

3

A Prodigious Index Finger

> In this connection one might recall John the Baptist in Grünewald's Crucifixion, especially his prodigious index finger. Could anyone point away from himself more impressively and completely (*illum oportet crescere me autem minui*)?[4]

++++

The painter Matthias Grünewald (ca. 1480–1528) painted the *Crucifixion* as part of the *Isenheim Altarpiece* in the hospital chapel of St. Anthony's Monastery (see xx). Here Jesus is on the cross at the center of the painting. To the right is John the Baptist. John holds an open book and is pointing to the crucified Christ. In the background in Latin, John's words are quoted: "He must increase, but I must decrease" (John 3:30). At John's feet we see a lamb with a cross. This reminds us of John's words at Jesus' baptism: "Here is the Lamb of God who takes away the sin of the world!" (John 1:29).

Barth kept a reproduction of this painting over his desk. He wrote of it in his *Church Dogmatics,* and noted the Baptist's "prodigious index finger" pointing to Christ. Barth saw this as what the biblical writers did. They pointed away from themselves toward Jesus Christ, the crucified Son of God. Just as John stood between the prophets of the Old Testament and the apostles of the New Testament, so the biblical writers, like John, pointed away from themselves. They were witnesses to God's revelation in the crucified Christ, the "Lamb of God who takes away the sin of the world."

4. Barth, *Church Dogmatics* I/1, 112. On the altarpiece, see the Wikipedia entry (https://en.wikipedia.org/wiki/Isenheim_Altarpiece). Barth's desk and the Grünewald painting are in Barbour Library at Pittsburgh Theological Seminary in Pittsburgh, Pennsylvania.

The biblical writers witnessed to what God had done in Jesus Christ. For Barth, the Scriptures pointed away from their words themselves to the reality of Jesus Christ. The Bible becomes the word of God for us when Scripture's words and message are received in faith and take on authority in our lives. Follow the "prodigious index finger!"

4

God Revealed

> God is who he is in his works[;] . . . in his works he is himself revealed as the one he is.[5]

+++++

Karl Barth always stresses that God is a God who *acts*. We can think abstractly about "God." Indeed, "God is"—that is basic, as Barth notes.

But God is who God is in God's act of revelation. God reveals God's self in what God *does*. In the Scriptures, God is shown as seeking and establishing a relationship between God and humans. "God is who he is in his works," said Barth. God is still who God is—even if God did no works. God is not diminished or lessened by acting. While God's works are bound to God, God is not bound to the works of God. God's works would be nothing without God. But God is who God is, even without God's works.

This means God is not who God is only in God's works. Yet also, God is not another than who God is in God's works. There is no wedge between who God is and what God does. The God we know in God's works is truly who God is. God's works reveal who God is.

These rather technical comments are actually quite important to us. On our own, we have no way of knowing God as God is. We cannot climb a ladder into heaven, pull back the clouds, and gaze on God's face. If we are to know God, it is God who must make the first move. God must reveal God's self to us.

This is what God has done. In Scripture we see God establishing relationships with people. God is revealed! God is revealed in God's works and actions. Supremely: God is revealed in God's Son, Jesus Christ. God's word has become a human being!

5. Barth, *Church Dogmatics* II/1, 260.

5
I Believe

> "I believe" means "I trust." No more must I dream of trusting in myself, I no longer require to justify myself, to excuse myself, to attempt to save and preserve myself. . . . I believe—not in myself—I believe in God the Father, the Son, and the Holy Ghost.[6]

++++

We sometimes hear that a person has trust issues. That's a way of saying it is difficult for one person to trust another in many contexts of life.

When it comes to Christian faith, "faith" in the biblical sense means "trust." Trust is relying on the faithfulness of another. We trust their promises, and believe what they ask of us is important. Primarily in the Scriptures, humans trust God. We rely on God's faithfulness and trust God's promises. We obey God as what is most important in our lives.

Barth saw faith as trust: "'I believe' means 'I trust.'" Our ultimate trust is in God; which frees us from dreaming about trust in ourselves, from trying to justify ourselves, or trying to excuse ourselves. In trust, we believe in *God*—not in our own powers or efforts. This means we do not need to try to save and preserve ourselves. Our faith and trust is in the triune God: "I believe—not in myself—I believe in God the Father, the Son, and the Holy Ghost." Trust in all other powers or authorities or other "gods" is "frail and superfluous"[7] according to Barth. In faith, we are delivered from trusting any other gods or powers.

6. Barth, *Dogmatics in Outline*, 18.

7. Barth, *Dogmatics in Outline*, 19.

We receive all things from our faithful God so we can be fully active for God. This what it means to believe. Our trust leads to lives of obedience and service to the living God!

6

Speaking of God

> Speaking of God means something *other than* speaking about the human in a somewhat higher pitch.[8]

++++

Theologians must speak of God.

That may sound self-evident. If theology is the study of God, then those who are theologians must engage in God-talk or the pursuit of the knowledge of God.

But the question is: *How* then do we speak of God? Questions throng.

In a 1922 lecture, Barth spoke of "The Word of God as the Task of Theology." Here he said theology must speak of God in the "foreground" and not the "background." By this he meant Christian theology must be primarily centered on God—the God of the Scriptures, which witness to God's revelation of God's self in God's Son, Jesus Christ. Jesus Christ, the Word of God, is the center of theology. Theology does not focus on the "divinization of the human" but on the incarnation of God.[9]

In this lecture, Barth countered the nineteenth-century theologian Friedrich Schleiermacher (1768–1834). Schleiermacher reoriented the theology of his time to human experience of God and piety. This, he believed, formed a basis for religious faith.

But Barth disagreed. He spoke clearly in leaving Schleiermacher out of the list of theologians he would recommend. For Barth, Schleiermacher had confused anthropology and theology. Famously, Barth said: "Speaking of God means something *other*

8. Barth, *Word of God and Theology*, 183 (italics his), from a 1922 lecture titled "The Word of God as the Task of Theology." The older translation of this lecture is in *Word of God and the Word*, 183–217, as "The Word of God and the Task of the Ministry." The quote cited from this translation is on page 196.

9. Barth, *Word of God and Theology*, 186.

than speaking about the human in a somewhat higher pitch." Or, in an older translation: "One can *not* speak of God simply by speaking of man in a loud voice." It is not the God-consciousness of humans that matters, it is God and God's self-revelation in Jesus Christ. This is how theology should speak of God: "Jesus Christ!"

7

Creation and Covenant

> The covenant is the goal of creation and creation the way to the covenant.[10]

++++

Karl Barth expressed the closest relationship between creation and covenant. The key to both is Jesus Christ. From Christ, we learn who God is as Creator, what God does, and what God's creatures are. We know this from Christ because Jesus Christ is the Word of God by which God has made, upholds, and renews creation. We know this by faith, the decision to recognize God's creation and God's lordship over all creation.

Theologically, Barth devoted long sections of his *Church Dogmatics* to two points. The first is that creation is the "external basis of the covenant."[11] Humans—and all reality—are created by God. In love, God wills to love and creates creatures to express and participate in love, expressed in God's covenant of grace in Jesus Christ. God's covenant rests on creation.

Second, the covenant is the "internal basis of creation."[12] What God intended in creation was that the covenant be the goal of creation. So creation was necessary and possible to establish the covenant God wished to initiate with humanity. Jesus Christ is the beginning of creation and also the goal of creation.

Put succinctly, Barth wrote that "the covenant is the goal of creation and creation the way to the covenant." This helps us see creation and covenant in important perspectives. God's creation opens the way to God's covenant, which is the goal of God's creative, loving actions. Creation is not the act of some super, faceless

10. Barth, *Church Dogmatics* III/1, 97.

11. Barth, *Church Dogmatics* III/1, 94–228.

12. Barth, *Church Dogmatics* III/1, 228–339.

power. Creation is the action of the God of Jesus Christ who desires, in love, to reach out to creatures and establish a covenant relationship with them, one fulfilled in Jesus Christ.

All creation points us toward Christ. Jesus Christ is the "divine Yes"[13] to God's glorious creation!

13. Barth, *Church Dogmatics* III/1, 385.

8

God Loves in Freedom

> God's being consists in the fact that he is the one who loves in freedom.[14]

++++

There are many definitions of God. We can speak of God in many ways. The Bible shows God's acts in creation, history, and in the lives of humanity. So there are many images to choose from if we ask, "Who is God?"

A basic description of God in Barth's theology is this: "God's being consists in the fact that he is the one who loves in freedom." "God is love" says the Scriptures (1 John 4:8, 16). This love, says Barth, is God's freely chosen way of being and is expressed in God's actions. Barth says God is the "perfect being," the "being which is itself perfection." This perfection is the perfection of perfect love in God's essence or being and in God's activities where God willingly enters into fellowship with God's creatures. This is how we humans know what love is: we see what God has done as the expression of who God is. God loves us humans in freedom—without regard to our worthiness or readiness or suitability. There is nothing to force God to love us. God freely loves us—because this is who God is!

There are a number of dimensions of God's love in freedom that make God's love the deepest reality we know in life. God's love is gracious—seeking us, freely. God's love is merciful and righteous—granting us mercy while calling for our obedience, freely. God's love is patient—not bringing us to account as soon as we sin, but kindly seeking to lead us to repentance (Rom 2:4). These and many other aspects are ways we experience God's loving us in freedom.

God chooses to love us, freely. Rejoice!

14. Barth, *Church Dogmatics* II/1, 322.

9

The Heart of the Christian Message

> Our starting point is that this "God with us" at the heart of the Christian message is the description of an act of God, or better, of God himself in this act of his.[15]

++++

Members of the Christian community, the church, have received a message. This message is the core of the Christian message. Members of the church share this message with the world.

The message is: "God with us." God is with you. God is with you and you and you. God is with us—the whole world! God is with even those who do not yet know this message. This is what Barth called "the decisive general statement of the Christian community."[16] The message is addressed to all people. It is carried throughout the world by those who have received it and are committed to sharing this message with all persons.

This message all has to do with God. It is *God* who is with us, *as God*. This is the center of the Christian message. The focus is on God and what God has done: coming to be with us as God's creatures. In the Scriptures, the name Emmanuel means "God with us." This was mentioned by the prophet Isaiah (7:14; 8:8, 10) and is seen as finding its fulfillment in the name of Jesus who will "save his people from their sins" (Matt 1:21). Jesus is Emmanuel, "which means, 'God is with us'" (1:23).

"God is with us" is "at the heart of the Christian message." It is, says Barth, "the description of an act of God, or better, of God himself in this act of his." This act of God, "God is with us," has a human name and is a human person: Jesus.

The church proclaims Jesus as "God with us"—the message for all the world!

15. Barth, *Church Dogmatics* IV/1, 6. See 4–6.

16. Barth, *Church Dogmatics* IV/1, 4.

10

Election of Grace: The Sum of the Gospel

> The election of grace is the sum of the gospel—we must put it as pointedly as that. But more, the election of grace is the whole of the gospel, the gospel *in nuce*. It is the very essence of all good news. . . . In the light of this election the whole of the gospel is light. Yes is said here, and all the promises of God are Yea and Amen (2 Cor 1:20).[17]

++++

Barth's doctrine or election (or predestination) was one of his most important theological contributions. He recast the traditional doctrine of election, which speaks of God's electing some for salvation while others are passed over or left in their own sins and face eternal separation from God.

Barth focused on God's election of grace, God's decision to be for humanity in the person of God's Son, Jesus Christ. This election of humanity to be in relation with God is seen in God's sending Jesus Christ, moving toward the world, to provide salvation—reconciliation of God with sinners. God's grace in sending Jesus Christ is the supreme expression of God's love. God says, "Yes" to sinners, and not "No." God loves sinners, who are elected in Jesus Christ, who himself is both the electing God and the first elected human. For Barth, "the divine salvation revealed in Jesus Christ is the place where the basis of the election is to be found."[18]

This is why Barth can refer to election by God's grace as "the sum of the gospel." This is the whole gospel in a nutshell. It is the essence of all "good news"—what can be greater than God's electing love for the world in Jesus Christ? All the gospel is light! All God's promises are fulfilled in Christ (2 Cor 1:20). God elects us; God is for us; God loves us!

17. Barth, *Church Dogmatics* II/2, 13–14.

18. Barth, *Church Dogmatics* II/1, 74.

11

Christ's Divinity in His Humanity

> The God who acts and speaks in Jesus Christ expresses his own true divinity precisely in his true humanity.[19]

+++++

God exists for the world, said Barth. God is in relationship with the world and its people. God is *for* the world and this is expressed supremely in God's decision to send Jesus Christ into the world: "The Word became flesh and lived among us" (John 1:14). God became a human person in Jesus Christ.

The Christian church has maintained that Jesus Christ is truly divine and truly human. He is one person in two natures. This is a true incarnation: God becoming fully and completely a human being. There were some in the early church who emphasized either the divinity or the humanity of Jesus, but the church has maintained both are found in Jesus Christ as the true incarnation of God.

Barth emphasized that "the God who acts and speaks in Jesus Christ expresses his own true divinity precisely in his true humanity." God's divinity is not abstract, theoretical, removed from human life. The divine Word—God!—expresses this divinity "precisely in his true humanity." The man, Jesus of Nazareth, was "God with us"—and with us *in* Jesus' humanity. God is so much for the world, that God became a person in the world and Jesus gave his life for the sake of the world.

Barth made this point in a 1956 lecture on the humanity of God. He said, "It is when we look at Jesus Christ that we know decisively that God's deity does not exclude, but includes his

19. Barth, *Church Dogmatics* IV/3/2, 763.

humanity."[20] We know God through Jesus—divinity expressed in humanity. Look to Jesus!

Jesus: God w/ us
— a contrast w/ creed

20. From Barth's lecture, "The Humanity of God" in *Humanity of God*, 49.

12

Christ's Death Fulfills the Incarnation

> His death on the cross was and is the fulfillment of the incarnation of the Word and therefore the humiliation of the Son of God and exaltation of the Son of Man.[21]

++++

The cross is central to Christianity because it is on the cross that the truly divine and truly human Jesus Christ—who was the incarnate Son of God—died for the sins of the world. He was "the Lamb of God who takes away the sin of the world" (John 1:29).

Jesus was God's Word made flesh (John 1:14) in the incarnation—God becoming human in Jesus Christ. Barth emphasized that the fulfillment of the incarnation, the completion of its purpose, is with Christ's death on the cross.

Theologians speak of Christ's humiliation as his becoming human, in which he remained obedient to God throughout his life. In this, Jesus' true humanity as the Son of God was expressed. Jesus' obedience extended to his death; as Paul put it: "he humbled himself and became obedient to the point of death—even death on a cross" (Phil 2:8).

In his cross, Christ reigns, and, as Jesus told his disciples, "Thus it is written, that the Messiah is to suffer and to rise from the dead on the third day" (Luke 24:26). Jesus' resurrection, ascension, and reign at the right hand of God is his exaltation. Jesus is supremely exalted and triumphant as "the Son of Man" (Mark 16:19; Rom 8:34).

God is revealed in Jesus Christ who died and was raised by the power of God. His incarnation is fulfilled by his resurrection and exaltation. This completed Jesus' messianic work. The

21. Barth, *Church Dogmatics* IV/2, 140–41.

reconciliation of the world was accomplished. We are now the new, true human beings we were created to be—in Jesus Christ!

13

Jesus Christ Is the Kingdom of God

> Jesus Christ is himself the established kingdom of God. And the establishment of this kingdom, the restoration of the relationship between himself and the creature, was the will of God from the beginning, the content of divine predestination.[22]

++++

The New Testament proclaims the message of the kingdom of God. It tells of the kingdom's reality and says "the kingdom of God has come near" (Mark 1:15). The time is fulfilled. The coming of the kingdom is the source of the whole New Testament message.

God's reign or kingdom has two dimensions. The kingdom is future. Its fullness will come when God's plan is fulfilled. We acknowledge this when we pray the Lord's Prayer: "your kingdom come" (Matt 6:10). This is the final, ultimate establishment of God's reign "forever and ever" (Rev 11:15).

But the New Testament also proclaims the kingdom has now come—in Jesus Christ. Jesus proclaimed the kingdom . . . and is himself God's kingdom. Barth said, "Jesus Christ is himself the established kingdom of God. And the establishment of this kingdom, the restoration of the relationship between himself and the creature, was the will of God from the beginning, the content of divine predestination." Early church theologians such as Origen said God's kingdom is a "self-kingdom"[23] (Greek *autobasileía*)—Jesus Christ is the kingdom *in himself*.

22. Barth, *Church Dogmatics* II/2, 177.

23. On Origen's use of this term, see Sanders, "Kingdom in Person." See also O'Collins, Jesus, 34, and Matthew 24:7 and 18:23. Barth quoted the early church theologian, Tertullian: "'In the gospel Christ Himself is the kingdom of God' (Adv. Marc., IV, xxiii, 8)" (*Christian Life*, 252).

Jesus came to restore the relationship between God and humanity. This was God's will from the beginning—what God chose to do in election or predestination. By faith, we recognize the reality of who Jesus is and what he has done. When we are reconciled to God in Christ and confess "Jesus is Lord" (1 Cor 12:3), we are free to pray and live with a view of the coming of the new heaven and new earth (Rev 21:1).

14
Gospel and Law

> The Creed is always at the same time the gospel, God's glad tidings to man, the message of Immanuel, God with us, to us; and as such it is necessarily also the law. Gospel and law are not to be separated; they are one, in such a way that the gospel is the primary thing, that the glad tidings are first in the field and, as such, include the law.[24]

++++

Martin Luther emphasized the Bible contained two types of statements: law and gospel. First, the law shows us humans that we are sinners. We stand condemned by God's law, which requires our obedience. As sinners, we cannot obey God's law perfectly or rightly. Only then, taught Luther, can we be ready to hear the gospel of God's love in Jesus Christ, which can bring us salvation.

Barth reversed Luther's formula. Gospel precedes law. Why? Because first and foremost, God has acted in Jesus Christ. God has decided to be with and for humanity by sending the Word-made-flesh to be a pure gift of grace.

This is what Barth described as God's "glad tidings" to us. Jesus Christ is "Immanuel, God with us, to us." This gospel of God's grace in Christ includes the law, which Jesus obeyed and fulfilled. In Jesus Christ there is forgiveness of sins. God speaks "Yes," where in the law we hear "No." Jesus bears the curse and consequences of human disobedience to God's law through his death on the cross. God's profound mercy in Christ justifies the sinner and establishes us as a "new creation" (2 Cor 5:17). Now, believers can receive the law as a gift, living joyfully in fellowship and obedience, serving God out of profound gratitude for God's grace in Jesus Christ.

24. Barth, *Dogmatics in Outline*, 19.

15

Only by Grace

It is by grace and *only* by grace that we are accepted by God.[25]

++++

The sixteenth-century Protestant Reformation centers on the theological insight that we receive salvation by "justification through faith alone." The shorthand, Latin "bumper sticker" was *sola fide*. We are saved by faith alone.

Barth indicated the meaning of this insight when he discussed the question of how we are righteous before God (Question 60 of the Heidelberg Catechism).

Basic here is the recognition that the ground of our confidence for salvation is not our good works. Nothing we try to do or accomplish in life can make us worthy of standing as justified people in God's sight. We are sinful people. All our good works are corrupted by our self-interest, our pride, our "turning in upon ourselves"[26]—a description by Luther for our sinful, human condition. God is perfect; we are not perfect. God is holy; we are not holy. We have broken God's divine law. None of our good works can merit our righteousness. So, says Barth, "It is by grace and *only* by grace that we are accepted by God."

God's grace is God's favor and love given to us in Jesus Christ. It is not a favor or love we can deserve or earn. All we can do is confess our sinfulness, believe, and trust in God's promise to forgive us in Jesus Christ who died for us. The righteousness, holiness, and obedience of Jesus Christ is ours, through faith—believing that Christ died for us. The one in whom we believe and trust, Jesus

25. Barth, *Heidelberg Catechism for Today*, 92 (italics his).

26. See Luther, *Luther's Works* (St. Louis), 25:345. Cf. McKim, *Moments with Martin Luther*, 9.

Christ, is the one who gives his righteousness to us so we can be forgiven, reconciled, and made new persons in the sight of God. Only by God's grace do we hear, "You are accepted!"

16

Grace Overcomes All Unworthiness

> Grace is the distinctive mode of God's being in so far as it seeks and creates fellowship by its own free inclination and favor, unconditioned by any merit or claim in the beloved, but also unhindered by any unworthiness or opposition in the latter—able, on the contrary, to overcome all unworthiness and opposition.[27]

++++

When we think of God, we should think of grace.

Barth believed grace is "the distinctive mode of God's being." Grace is "an inner mode of being in God Himself." This means that what is most essential, most characteristic, most definitive about God is . . . God's grace.

This grace "seeks and creates fellowship by its own free inclination." God's grace is freely given. God's grace is freely given as love by God. For Barth, "the love of God is grace." Grace is God's seeking of fellowship with humans. It is God's favor purely and freely given to humans. We do not deserve God's grace. If we deserved grace, it would not be grace—it would be merit.

God's freely given grace, expressed as love, is not something we can claim for ourselves. God's freely given grace is received as God's gift to us. We receive fellowship with our Creator, because God desires to express God's love ("God loves in freedom," said Barth—see #8 above). God desires to express God's love in grace despite our unworthiness (as sinners) to be objects of God's love; or, even when we oppose and reject God's loving grace (as sinners).

27. Barth, *Church Dogmatics*, II/1, 353.

But God's grace overcomes the opposition of sin. Our feelings of unworthiness are removed. Our self-love is directed to love of God. God overcomes our unworthiness through grace, by grace. God gives the gift of God's own self in Jesus Christ. In Jesus we receive God's grace!

17

Grace Greater Than Our Sin

> We are forbidden to take sin more seriously than grace, or even as seriously as grace.[28]

++++

Christian theology affirms, and Barth continually emphasized, the seriousness of human sin. The attitudes of fallen humanity toward God—in rejecting God's love, living in disobedience, and turning away from God's purposes—break the relationship of trust and love God desired in creation for the divine/human relationship. Humans sin against God's grace and know our sinful nature only in relation to God's grace. We see our sinful nature most clearly in Jesus, who reveals the word of God and shows us the nature of humanity as created by God.

But in the midst of human sinfulness, God maintains the freedom to be a gracious God to human sinners. God became a human in Jesus Christ and God's word becomes the gospel of Jesus Christ. In Christ, we see the revelation of God's attitude toward sin: sin is of terrible gravity; sin cannot be atoned for by sinful persons; sin incurs God's judgment. But there is more . . . .

The good news of the gospel is that God delivers us! God saves us by judging our sin in Jesus Christ. So, "we are forbidden to take sin more seriously than grace, or even as seriously as grace." God's grace is primary; human sin is secondary. God's grace is greater than our sin.

At times, we experience the severe weight of sin in our lives. We may feel that when it comes to sinners, "I am the foremost" (1 Tim 1:15). But Barth urges us to keep things in perspective. God's grace is primary . . . and dominant. Jesus is victor! Jesus overcomes sin and death. This is the triumph of God's grace!

28. Barth, *Church Dogmatics* III/2, 41.

In the midst of our dark night of the soul, we can hold to the reality that God's grace is greater than all our sin.

18

The Wonderful Exchange

> There is an exchange of status between him and us: His righteousness and holiness are ours, our sin is his; he is lost for us, and we for his sake are saved. By this exchange ([Greek: καταλλαγή; reconciliation] 2 Cor 5:19) revelation stands or falls.[29]

++++

We cannot save ourselves. We cannot overcome the sin that separates us from God and from others. This sin is of our own fault. But we cannot simply pronounce ourselves to be just or clean or redeemed from this situation. If we try this approach, we are lying—to ourselves and God. For when we look at God—as we know God in Jesus Christ—we find we will always fall far short of who God wants us to be and who God created us to be as God's children.

But Jesus Christ gives us what we cannot achieve or sustain for ourselves. Instead of leaving us to try to reconcile ourselves to God, Jesus Christ brings reconciliation of God with the world by giving up himself. We receive this reconciliation as a gift of God's grace. Everything is done for us—in Christ. He is the assistance that comes to us. He is God's word spoken to us. As Barth puts it: "There is an exchange of status between him and us: His righteousness and holiness are ours, our sin is his; he is lost for us, and we for his sake are saved. By this exchange ([Greek: καταλλαγή; reconciliation] 2 Cor 5:19) revelation stands or falls."

This is the "wonderful exchange"[30] of which Martin Luther spoke. Christ exchanges his righteousness for our sin, bearing on

29. Barth, *Church Dogmatics* I/2, 308.

30. See Luther, *Luther's Works* (Philadelphia), 51:316. Cf. McKim, *Moments with Martin Luther*, 18.

himself the sin of the world. Christ's righteousness and holiness become ours through faith and by grace.

Praise Christ! Rejoice in this wonderful exchange for our salvation!

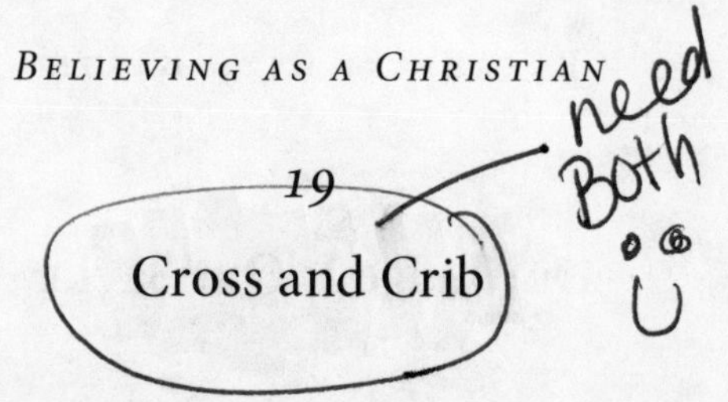

19

Cross and Crib

> Except we see the cross of Golgotha, we cannot hear the gospel at the crib of Bethlehem.[31]

++++

The cross of Golgotha, on which Jesus Christ died, effected the reconciliation of the world to God. This is the great, central event for human salvation. Without the cross, there is no redemption and the world remains in its sin.

The crib of Bethlehem is where the Savior of the world, Jesus Christ, was born. He is Emmanuel, "God with us." He is the divine Word of God. He is the revelation of God, the "Word made flesh" (John 1:14). Without the crib at Bethlehem, God and the world would be permanently estranged.

Barth emphasized the importance of Good Friday and Christmas when he wrote that "except we see the cross of Golgotha, we cannot hear the gospel at the crib of Bethlehem." The death of Jesus and the birth of Jesus are both crucial and essential. Jesus was born with a purpose. Jesus was born to die. Jesus said, "I came not to judge the world, but to save the world" (John 12:47). In Jesus Christ, we see God is for us as humans. God did not give up on the sinful humans who willfully rebelled against their Creator. Instead, out of love, God gave the "only Son," Jesus Christ, to reveal God's will and reconcile the world in salvation (John 3:16). This is the gospel!

Cross and crib go together. Without the cross, there would be no salvation for humanity. Without the crib there would be no revelation of God. The miracle of Christmas is that God has become a human being in Jesus Christ. On the cross, Jesus obediently suffered death so the heart of God's love could be revealed. Cross and crib!

31. Barth, *Christmas*, 13.

20

Our Judge Is Our Savior

> All men (we too!) are his enemies—but that we all go to meet the Judge who gave himself for us. It is true that he is the *Judge*; there can be no doctrine of universal salvation. Nevertheless, he is the Judge whom we Christians may *know*.[32]

++++

In the Apostles' Creed, we confess we believe that Jesus Christ will return to judge the living and the dead. This is a statement about the future, referring to the so-called second coming of Christ.

Usually when we hear preachers preach about the second coming, we know we are in for some fearsome images and lots of talk about God's judgment.

It is true, said Barth, that Christ will return as the Judge. This is why, Barth said, there can be no doctrine of universal salvation. Yet there is something to remember here. Barth says that when Christians meet Christ as Judge, "he is the Judge whom we Christians may *know*." The same Jesus who is our future Judge is the same one who was judged for us, who died for us, who submitted himself to God's judgment for me on the cross. In short: the Judge is our Savior.

When we know Christ as the one who was judged and who died for us, we look forward to a future of joy and glory. Enemies of Christ—those who do not know of his saving death and love—will be judged. But we *know* our Judge. The one who judges us is the one who gave himself for us. Christ died for our sins.

We Christians confess and bear witness that Christ died for all—even for his enemies. We proclaim: Our Judge is our Savior!

32. Barth, *Heidelberg Catechism for Today*, 82 (italics his). Cf. Barth, *Dogmatics in Outline*, 134.

21

Jesus Was Judged in Our Place

> It is our basic sin to take the place of the Judge, to try to judge ourselves and others. All our other sins, both small and great, derive ultimately from this source. . . . [Jesus] took our place as Judge. He took our place as the judged. He was judged in our place. And he acted justly in our place.[33]

++++

When we live in sin, we make ourselves our own judge. We live however we want, and judge our actions according to our own self-interests. We also set ourselves up as the judge of others. Our sinfulness makes us the center of our universe, and what we want is the standard for assessing ourselves and condemning others. Barth recognized this when he wrote: "It is our basic sin to take the place of the Judge, to try to judge ourselves and others. All our other sins, both small and great, derive ultimately from this source."

But Jesus has come to be the Judge who is judged in our place. This is what happened in the cross of Christ. Jesus took the place of us sinners. Jesus came for us and died for us (Latin *pro nobis*) and for the world.

"Jesus took our place as Judge." Instead of setting ourselves up as judge over all, Jesus has come to take responsibility on himself as the pure, spotless Son of God. He takes on our own evilness, our sin.

"He took our place as the judged" and "was judged in our place." This is a substitutionary atonement. Jesus took the judgment for sin that we deserved.

"He acted justly in our place." Jesus' judgment for us reconciles us with God. Jesus, the innocent one, has died for the guilty ones.

Jesus did all this . . . for us!

33. Barth, *Church Dogmatics*, IV/1, 235, 273.

22

Jesus Christ Is the Atonement

> Jesus Christ is the atonement. But that means that he is the maintaining and accomplishing and fulfilling of the divine covenant as executed by God himself. He is the eschatological realization of the will of God for Israel and therefore for the whole race.[34]

++++

"Atonement" is an English-language term to describe the death of Jesus Christ. It means God and humans are "at-one" through Christ's death on the cross. It has Old Testament roots in the "Day of Atonement" (Hebrew *Yom Kippur*; Lev 16) when the high priest offered a sacrifice of atonement for the sins of Israel. Through Christ's death, human sin is forgiven as Jesus offered himself as the atoning sacrifice for the sins of the world.

Barth says that "Jesus Christ is the atonement." In another place, he wrote that "to say atonement is to say Jesus Christ."[35] Jesus is "the maintaining and accomplishing and fulfilling of the divine covenant" which God established and carried out. In the covenant, God is "for us" and provides for the forgiveness of sins through the Son of God who is "God with us." Jesus Christ is the "new covenant" (1 Cor 11:25).

Barth wrote that Jesus is "the eschatological realization of the will of God for Israel and therefore for the whole race." By this, Barth means that Jesus Christ as the atonement, the one who joins God and humanity in himself, reveals God's ultimate divine will for Israel and all humanity. Jesus is the covenant God established, God's desire for Israel and which was widened to include all persons. An eschatological realization is a fulfillment at the end of

34. Barth, *Church Dogmatics* IV/1, 34.

35. Barth, *Church Dogmatics* IV/1, 158.

time ("eschatology" or "the last things"). By his atoning death, Jesus carries out what God has intended—stretching to the end of the world!

23

Christ Is Our Hope

> Our sole future is that *He* will come, just as our sole present is that he has come. By virtue of his kingly office, as that became visible in his resurrection, the church is in the position of having no other future than that which it acknowledges in the prayer: Amen; come, Lord Jesus! By virtue of his kingly office it *has* this future. *Venturus est* [he will come] therefore means: Christ is our *hope*, and *Christ* is our hope.[36]

++++

In the Apostles' Creed, we confess: "He will come again." We affirm what Jesus promised: "I will come again and will take you to myself" (John 14:3). This is our future. We live into this future as surely as we live in the present—that Jesus Christ is "God with us" and has lived among us. He has come!

In his resurrection, affirmed in the phrase before "He will come again," we see Jesus Christ as the Victor, the King over death and all other powers in the universe. In the church we proclaim Jesus Christ is Lord of all and King of all. This is the church's future for which we pray: "Amen; come, Lord Jesus" (Rev 22:20)! This is our prayer for the reality into which we live: Jesus will come again and is now King of the cosmos!

Barth explained these realities and wrote: "*Venturus est* [he will come] therefore means: Christ is our *hope*, and *Christ* is our hope." He emphasizes that Christ is our hope and that it is Christ who is our hope.

In Christ, we share the hope of "sharing the glory of God" (Rom 5:2). Only Christ gives this gift to us. Eternal life with the all-glorious God is ours!

36. Barth, *Credo*, 120 (italics his).

24

God Looks at Us through Christ

> If God knows humanity, if he sees us and judges us, it is always through the person of Jesus Christ, his own Son, who has been obedient and is the object of his delight. By Jesus Christ, humanity is in the presence of God. God looks at Christ, and it is through him that he looks at us. We have, therefore, a representative before God.[37]

++++

The work of Jesus Christ in dying for us brings us salvation. Our sin is forgiven and we are reconciled with God. God's electing purposes are enacted through Jesus Christ. We know God through Christ. Christ has carried out God's redemptive purposes for us and the judgment for sin that we deserve has been taken on by the innocent Son of God. In this, Jesus "humbled himself and became obedient to the point of death—even death on a cross" (Phil 2:8).

Jesus Christ has revolutionized our lives! Now we can live "in the presence of God." As Barth says, "God looks at Christ, and it is through him that he looks at us. We have, therefore, a representative before God."

As those reconciled to God in Christ, God now views us through Jesus Christ and what Christ has done for us. God does not see us as hostile enemies. Now we are friends again with God, through the work of God's Son. Now God sees us through the work of Christ, as those united to Christ by faith. God sees us as righteous in that we are clothed in the righteousness of Christ.

Now we have a representative before God. Christ, who died for us, now stands before God to represent us. Now we have an "advocate with the Father, Jesus Christ the righteous" (1 John 2:1). We can now pray through Jesus Christ. All our prayers are summed up in him!

37. Barth, *Prayer*, 14.

25

Christ Reigns from the Cross

His resurrection revealed him as the one who reigns in virtue of his death, from the cross (*regnantem in cruce*).[38]

++++

In the New Testament, Jesus' cross and resurrection go together. Each is crucial to the work of Jesus Christ.

The whole New Testament points to Jesus' death as the beginning of the new beginnings God established. By Christ's death, the world is reconciled to God. The world has a new beginning. By Christ's death, humans are changed from sinners to righteous in Jesus Christ. Humans are restored to the relationship with God intended in their creation. They are justified, set right with God through Christ's death. They are sanctified, they grow in God's grace. They are exalted into becoming a true covenant partner with God. In Christ's cross, Barth emphasized, the crucified is also the Lord and King of all persons. God's kingdom is inaugurated in history.

Christ reigns from the cross! This is what the resurrection revealed. Said Barth: "His resurrection revealed him as the one who reigns in virtue of his death, from the cross (*regnantem in cruce*)." The resurrection shows the power of the cross to make all things new (2 Cor 5:17)!

Christ's reign from the cross establishes God's new creation through all the earth. The world is now fundamentally different, it has been reconciled to God through the death of Christ. Those who recognize Christ's reign from the cross, by faith, are those who are ruled by Christ because we too have "died with Christ"

38. Barth, *Church Dogmatics* IV/2, 291.

(Rom 6:8). We now live as God's covenant partners, disciples of Jesus Christ, and are his witnesses in the world. In the torturous execution Jesus experienced, the power of God's saving love defeated evil and death. Christ reigns from the cross!

Jesus' death is
beginnin of new beginnings...

to be justified.. to be made right w/God

Christ reeigns from the cross
power of cross to make all things new

26
The Great Verdict of God

> The resurrection of Jesus Christ is the great verdict of God, the fulfillment and proclamation of God's decision concerning the event of the cross.[39]

+++++

Every Lord's Day worship service celebrates the day of resurrection. The Christian community gathers around its risen Lord: Jesus Christ has been raised by the power of God!

Worship centers in the resurrection because, as Barth wrote, "The resurrection of Jesus Christ is the great verdict of God, the fulfillment and proclamation of God's decision concerning the event of the cross." Jesus Christ "became obedient to the point of death—even death on a cross" (Phil 2:8). His death "fulfilled the divine wrath," said Barth, but did so "in the service of the divine grace." God accepts Christ's death as an act that judges the world, "but judges it with the aim of saving it," Barth proclaims.

In the cross and resurrection, God has expressed a "Yes" to reconciling the world. The resurrection is God's great verdict of "Yes" to the cross as the means of salvation. The event of Jesus' resurrection on Easter Day "revealed and confirmed and brought into effect"[40] the event of Good Friday. Now, we are forever treated by God as those for whom Jesus Christ died and was raised! He was "raised for our justification" (Rom 4:25). God's verdict for us is "Yes"!

Whenever we worship and praise the resurrected Christ, we receive the gracious benefits of what Christ has done as the living Word of God. We commit our whole selves in obedience to serving God in Christ. We are Jesus' disciples. We are Easter people—those

39. Barth, *Church Dogmatics* IV/1, 309.

40. Barth, *Church Dogmatics* IV/1, 313.

who live with Jesus Christ in our midst now, and live knowing that the future of the world is secure in the risen Christ, the Lord of time, and "the God of our salvation" (Ps 65:5).

27

The Meaning of Salvation

> Salvation means therefore not merely that man is saved from certain very serious consequences of his sin, or merely that his original relation to God is restored. Beyond all this, salvation means that man becomes a new man. This new man is the man who in God's sight is not a sinner but a righteous being, and therefore one who has escaped from death and partakes of life.[41]

++++

Salvation as God's reconciliation of humanity with God by the death and resurrection of Jesus Christ has many facets. Foremost, theologically, salvation is the work of God, not the work of humans. Only God could send Jesus Christ to forgive the sin of the world and bring communion and fellowship with God.

Salvation includes humans not receiving the consequences of our sin, while receiving the restoration of the relationship with God we were created to have. But salvation also means, says Barth, that humans become new persons (Eph 2:15), termed by Paul as "a new creation: everything old has passed away; see, everything has become new" (2 Cor 5:17)!

Barth says the new person in Jesus Christ is seen by God as "not a sinner but a righteous being, and therefore one who has escaped from death and partakes of life." This new life in Christ is lived in union with Christ by the power of the Spirit. We are members of the body of Christ, the church (1 Cor 12:27), serving Christ in ongoing ministries sustained by lives of prayer and "a living hope through the resurrection of Jesus Christ from the dead" (1 Pet 1:3). This is the meaning of salvation!

41. Barth, *Knowledge of God*, 81.

28

Ascension—Time of Great Opportunity

> We may name this time which broke in with Jesus Christ's ascension into heaven, "the time of the Word." . . . It is the time in which the church is united with Christ only in faith and by the Holy Spirit; it is the interim time between his earthly existence and his return in glory; it is the time of the great opportunity, of the task of the church towards the world; it is the time of mission.[42]

++++

The ascension of Jesus into heaven after his resurrection (Acts 1:6–11) marked the end of Jesus' time on earth. It is a time of his absence from earth, and yet continuing to be present by the power of the word of God and the work of the Holy Spirit. As Barth wrote, "We may name this time which broke in with Jesus Christ's ascension into heaven, 'the time of the Word.' . . . It is the time in which the church is united with Christ only in faith and by the Holy Spirit." It is an interim time as the church lives between the days of Jesus' earthly existence and looks forward to the day of Christ's "return in glory" (Matt 25:31; 1 Thess 4:13–18).

What do we do as we look back and look ahead?

Barth says this is a time of "great opportunity." Now the church carries out its task toward the world. Now God's mission in the world is carried out. We are cut in on the action, working to carry out God's purposes for the world in Jesus Christ. The risen, ascended Christ is with us; the Holy Spirit leads and guides us. The Christian community witnesses to God's work of salvation and is sent to serve the world in Jesus Christ. Now is the great opportunity!

42. Barth, *Dogmatics in Outline*, 128.

29

The Fellowship of the Holy Spirit

> The fellowship of the Holy Spirit is nothing other than the actually operative might and power of the work of the Lord Jesus Christ, which has become a word addressed to particular men and has awakened their answer. The fellowship of the Holy Spirit creates the living community.[43]

We are familiar with the benediction Paul wrote to the Corinthian Christians: "The grace of the Lord Jesus Christ, the love of God, and the communion of the Holy Spirit be with all of you" (2 Cor 13:13). The Greek word translated "communion" (Gk, κοινωνία; Lat. *koinōnia*) can also be translated "fellowship." In this quotation from Barth, "fellowship" is used.

"The fellowship of the Holy Spirit" is what Barth sees as the essence of the church. This fellowship is "the actually operative might and power of the work of the Lord Jesus Christ." Christ's might and power, expressed in his work, are put into effect by the Holy Spirit. The Spirit enables the benefits of what Jesus Christ did to address us as humans. We know of Jesus through the Spirit.

The Spirit also awakens our answer. What will we think of Christ? What will we do with Christ? Our response to the Spirit—by faith in believing in Jesus Christ—is the work of the Spirit. The Spirit makes the divine Word, Jesus, in his death and resurrection, become the divine word *to us*.

Barth says "the fellowship of the Holy Spirit creates the living community." "Church" is the content of this fellowship of the Holy Spirit as we are joined with others who say "Jesus Christ is Lord" (1 Cor 12:3). The fellowship of the Holy Spirit proceeds "from the very heart of God," said Barth, creating the living community of faith!

43. Barth, *God Here and Now*, 80.

30

The Spirit Witnesses to Jesus Christ

> It is divine witness—the witness of the Holy Spirit—in the fact that Jesus Christ is its power and light, its content, its origin and goal. It is the fulfillment of his self-witness.[44]

++++

Paul proclaimed that "no one can say 'Jesus is Lord' except by the Holy Spirit" (1 Cor 12:3). We confess Jesus Christ as Lord by the power of the Holy Spirit. The Spirit witnesses to Jesus Christ. This is the work of the Holy Spirit in establishing faith and directing faith to focus on Jesus Christ as God's self-revelation as the Savior of the world (1 John 4:14).

The Holy Spirit, in the New Testament, is a witness who points away from the Spirit to the Son, Jesus Christ. As Barth noted, the witness of the Spirit is in the fact that "Jesus Christ is its power and light, its content, its origin and goal." The Spirit's witness is "the fulfillment" of Christ's "self-witness." All Jesus said about himself—who he was and what he would do—is his attestation or witness to himself as the revelation of God.

The Holy Spirit in the here and now brings this witness "to life" for us, so to speak. The Spirit points us toward Jesus Christ. The Spirit does not witness to the Spirit, but *to Christ*, who is the power, light, content, origin, and goal of the Spirit's work.

This is the divine work of the Spirit totally apart from us. But the Spirit's work is for us in bringing us to the recognition of who Jesus is and what he has done for our salvation. The Spirit brings Jesus Christ into our personal lives. The Spirit inserts us into the Christian community. Faith happens to us by the witness of the Holy Spirit!

44. Barth, *Church Dogmatics*, IV/2, 130.

31

God's Great Lovingkindness

> This much is certain, that we have no theological right to set any sort of limits to the loving-kindness of God which has appeared in Jesus Christ. Our theological duty is to see and understand it as being still greater than we had seen before.[45]

++++

In the history of the church, there have always been those who have advocated universalism. This is the view that all persons will be saved. The argument is that God is love and loves all people. Therefore, God must give salvation to all persons, regardless of their lives or actions. Universalism has always been a strand of Christian belief; but never the "majority report."

Barth's theology, with its emphases on God's mercy on all persons, the universal atonement of Jesus Christ for human sin, and God's reconciliation of the world, have led some to say that Barth taught universalism.

Barth's theology does move in this direction. But, as some have said, Barth comes just to the brink of universalism. To insist God must save all people is to impose on the freedom of God to do what God purposes. Universalism cannot be made into a theological principle since it prescribes to God what God *must* do.

In discussing universalism, Barth said, "This much is certain, that we have no theological right to set any sort of limits to the loving-kindness of God which has appeared in Jesus Christ. Our theological duty is to see and understand it as being still greater than we had seen before."

What God does in salvation is *God's* choice. But we cannot set limits on God's loving-kindness. The God we know in Jesus Christ is a loving God. God's will shall be done!

45. Barth, *Humanity of God*, 62.

32

God's Mercy on All

> As according to God's Holy Word, spoken in Jesus Christ, he has mercy on all, each of you may and shall repeat—not after me, but after him—"I am one of them." God has mercy on me and will have mercy on me. . . . God has mercy on all, including you and me. As a result you and I may and shall live from this 'Yes' spoken to all men, spoken to us, and live here and now![46]

++++

On September 22, 1957, Karl Barth preached a sermon: "All!" to prisoners in the Basel jail. His text was Romans 11:32: "For God has imprisoned all in disobedience so that he may be merciful to all."

Barth proclaimed God's mercy is divine and is poured out on all persons. God's mercy is poured out on *all*—to the good and the evil alike. God mercy is truly extended to *all*. This is shown in the parables of the lost sheep, the lost coin, and the prodigal son (Luke 15).

This mercy may seem too wonderful to believe. So Barth said, "As according to God's Holy Word, spoken in Jesus Christ, he has mercy on all, each of you may and shall repeat—not after me, but after him—'I am one of them.' God has mercy on me and will have mercy on me. . . . God has mercy on all, including you and me." This makes God's mercy intimately personal. This is *God's* mercy. In the past God has had mercy on me; and in the future God will have mercy on me. God's mercy extends to all—to you and to me.

So we can live here and now hearing God's "Yes" spoken to us: God is merciful to all!

46. Barth, *Deliverance to the Captives*, 87.

33
This Is Reconciliation

> This is reconciliation: his damnation our liberation, his defeat our victory, his mortal pain the beginning of our joy, his death the birth of our life. We do well to remember that this is what those who put him to death really accomplished. They did not know what they did. These deluded men and women accomplished by their evil will and deed that good which God had willed and done with the world and for the world, including the crowd of Jerusalem.[47]

++++

On Good Friday, 1957, Barth preached in the Basel jail. His sermon was titled, "The Criminals with Him." He told the story of the crucifixion of Jesus and explained the meaning of that death—for criminals and for the whole world.

God has come into the world and taken on human nature. God became a human person in the man Jesus. In Jesus, God has delivered humans from evil and taken us to God's heart as the children of God, bringing us eternal life.

Jesus died on the cross where God has reconciled the world. In Christ, the "innocent took the place of us the guilty." In Jesus, our burden is removed as Christ took it upon himself. This is reconciliation. We have new life: "his damnation our liberation, his defeat our victory, his mortal pain the beginning of our joy, his death the birth of our life."

In the evil event of the death of Jesus, "that good which God had willed and done" with and for the world was carried out. Now we are liberated from sin, the power of death is broken, pain gives way to joy, and in Jesus' death is "the birth of our life." We are reconciled with God!

47. Barth, *Deliverance to the Captives*, 80.

34

Reconciliation of the World in Jesus Christ

> Here, in the world, there was revealed and made known in this event [the resurrection of Jesus Christ] what took place for the world in the life and death of Jesus Christ, namely, the alteration of the situation between God and the world by the reconciliation of the world to God accomplished in him.[48]

++++

A recurring theme for Barth is the reconciliation of the world in Jesus Christ. This is central to Christian faith and takes place through the cross and resurrection of Christ. God has spoken through the actions of Christ's death and his being raised by the power of God. These events have permanent, ever-lasting effects. They are done once for all and irrevocably. They are done for the sake of humanity, whether they are recognized as valid by individual persons or not.

Barth wrote: "Here, in the world, there was revealed and made known in this event [the resurrection] what took place for the world in the life and death of Jesus Christ, namely, the alteration of the situation between God and the world by the reconciliation of the world to God accomplished in him." In the resurrection, which vindicates his death on the cross, Christ is revealed to the world as the Word of God. The risen Christ is spoken and proclaimed to the world.

The effect of Christ's reconciling act is to change the state of the world—permanently. Now there is a new relationship between God and the world by the reconciliation accomplished in Christ. Barth said now that Christ is risen, no one "who has lived or will

48. Barth, *Church Dogmatics* IV/3/1, 298.

live is the same" as that person would have been "if Jesus Christ had not risen!" Reconciliation is publicly proclaimed and imparted. God is ever-faithful to the world and to us!

35

God Says "Yes"

> But because the risen and living Jesus Christ is the one Word of God, this Word—as the community hears and proclaims it—is the one Word of the divine will and act of reconciliation. It is God's Yes to man and the world, even in the No of the cross which it includes. God says No in order to say Yes. . . . The community lives by the fact that the first and final Word of God is this Yes.[49]

++++

By his death on the cross, Jesus showed the sinfulness of humanity and in himself absorbed the judgment on sin that humans deserve. Sin's power should have destroyed humanity fully and completely. Humans rebel against God. We assume in arrogance and pretension to judge ourselves—and to justify ourselves according to our own will and desires. The cross of Christ shows humans obstinately ignore and reject the truth of the word of God, thinking we can help ourselves, that our cause is God's cause. This is the judgment the cross of Christ brings to all humanity.

But there is more. Jesus was raised! The living Jesus Christ is "the one Word of God," said Barth, "this Word—as the community hears and proclaims it—is the one Word of the divine will and act of reconciliation." Jesus is raised so humans are not destroyed. We are saved!

Jesus Christ is "God's Yes to man and the world, even in the No of the cross which it includes. God says No in order to say Yes. . . . The community lives by the fact that the first and final Word of God is this Yes."

God wills that the "No" of the cross becomes the "Yes" of the resurrection. This "Yes" is God's ultimate word. God's saving word is "Yes!"

49. Barth, *Church Dogmatics* IV/1, 347.

36

God Loves All

> God is he who in his Son Jesus Christ loves all his children, in his children all men, and in men his whole creation. God's being is his loving. He is all that he is as the one who loves. All his perfections are the perfections of his love.[50]

++++

We know God's love not in the abstract—as a theory or concept—but concretely in God's Son, Jesus Christ. Most clearly, we know God's love in Jesus Christ by God's sending Jesus as God's revelation: "For God so loved the world that he gave his only Son, so that everyone who believes in him may not perish but may have eternal life" (John 3:16). This is God's unique love: Jesus Christ. As Barth notes, all love meets in the revelation and reconciliation Jesus Christ brings.

In Jesus Christ, God loves all of God's children and in God's children, all persons, and in them God's whole creation. God loves all! The God who loves the whole creation loves all persons in the whole creation.

"God's being is his loving," wrote Barth. This is God's nature. God is all God is "as the one who loves." This accords with the biblical message and the clear statement: "God is love" (1 John 4:8, 16). This is a primary word spoken to us. God's love for us is overwhelming, overflowing, and free, according to Barth. God's graciousness, mercy, and patience express God's loving. To put it more technically, all God's perfections are "the perfections of his love." God is loving within God's self and in all God's works.

Since God loves us, we love others (1 John 4:11). This is a command to love others who are of the household of faith, but even more, to extend love to all others—whoever they are. For God loves all!

50. Barth, *Church Dogmatics* II/1, 351.

37

The Earthly-Historical Form of Jesus Christ

> The community is the earthly-historical form of existence of Jesus Christ himself. . . . Because he is, it is; it is, because he is. That is its secret, its being in the third dimension, which is visible only to faith.[51]

++++

There are many New Testament images for the church. A few readily come to mind: The people of God; the body of Christ; the fellowship of the Holy Spirit. When we try to say "church," restricting ourselves to one image is inadequate!

When Barth described the church, as we confess in the Apostles' Creed, he tried to say what the nature of the Christian community was. He wanted to recognize the church's visible and historical form. But he also wanted to talk about a "third dimension," a theological dimension, to which the creed points. This theological dimension is visible only to faith. We can also see the church on the corner, or the congregation that gathers for 11 a.m. Sunday worship. But is there more?

Barth said the community is: "the earthly-historical form of existence of Jesus Christ himself . . . ." When we see church, we recognize this represents Jesus Christ's presence in human history today. No other group or organization makes that claim.

Barth went on to say that "Because he is, it is; it is, because he is. That is its secret, its being in the third dimension, which is visible only to faith." The church is grounded in Jesus Christ; the church's reason for being is Jesus Christ. This is its secret—Jesus Christ is present in the church! This presence of Christ is visible only to

51. Barth, *Church Dogmatics* IV/1, 661.

faith. By faith we perceive what Christ is doing in and through the church and its members. The church's members acknowledge what God has done in Christ—the Lord who became a servant.

38

Jesus Christ Is in Our Midst

> The Lord's Supper is quite simply the sign of what we have said: Jesus Christ is in our midst, he, the man in whom God himself has poured out his life for our sake and in whom our life is lifted up to God. Holy Communion is the sign that Jesus Christ is our beginning and we may rise up and walk into the future where we shall live. The Lord himself gives us strength, food, and drink for our journey, from *one* bread and from *one* cup, because he is one, he the one for us all.[52]

++++

Through the history of the church, there have been differing views about the Lord's Supper. Churches have been—and remain—divided over this issue.

Barth's view of baptism and the Lord's Supper evolved. But when he preached to prisoners in Basel's jail on Easter, 1955, he spoke simply about the Lord's Supper. He did not delve into theological theories. He said the Supper is a "sign" that "Jesus Christ is in our midst." Jesus is "the man in whom God himself has poured out his life for our sake"—the Supper pointing to the cross of Christ where Jesus died for the sins of the world (John 1:29).

The good news of Easter is that "our life is lifted up to God." For the Supper is also "the sign that Jesus Christ is our beginning and we may rise up and walk into the future where we shall live." For this journey into new life—marked by Jesus' resurrection—we are given strength, food, and drink for our journey. This comes to us from the bread and the cup—from "the one for us all"—Jesus Christ. He is in our midst!

52. Barth, *Deliverance to the Captives*, 33 (italics his).

LIVING AS A CHRISTIAN

39

We are Secure

> The security of the Christian is not that fancied by the Stoics. The Christian is secure, absolutely and essentially secure, because his life is hid with the risen Christ in God., i.e., with the one who was not overcome by the world but overcame it (Col 3:3).[1]

++++

Because Jesus Christ is risen, the future is already present here and now. This future of the world—and the Christian—secured in Jesus Christ, determines and shapes our lives every day. In the midst of afflictions, we have hope and security. We believe God's future is taking shape through the power of Christ's resurrection in our lives (Heb 6:5).

Nothing else can give us this security. The ancient Stoics believed humans should live by taking what fate gives them—"whatever will be, will be." There can be no trust one's life will not be destroyed or ruined or overthrown.

But, as Barth says: "The Christian is secure, absolutely and essentially secure, because his life is hid with the risen Christ in God., i.e., with the one who was not overcome by the world but overcame it (Col 3:3)." This is our hope and promise of security: "Your life is hidden with Christ in God" (Col 3:3). Our lives are

1. Barth, *Church Dogmatics* IV/3/2, 645.

secured in the power of God in Christ, in the risen Christ who has overcome the world (John 16:33).

Despite our afflictions, our difficulties, and the disturbances of life, we have absolute and complete security because Jesus Christ is risen! By faith, we are united to Christ and held secure by God's love for us in Christ: "If God is for us, who is against us" (Rom 8:31)? No person or force can "do us true and serious harm, or finally overcome us," said Barth. We are secure!

40

Back Home Again

> It is objectively the case that we are all away from home—exiles. In Jesus we are all back home again.[2]

++++

Humans are sinners. Barth has an extensive doctrine of sin which he sees in relation to Jesus Christ. In his *Church Dogmatics*, he discusses sin after he has discussed Christology—the doctrine of Jesus Christ. We sin in relation to Jesus and his reconciliation of humanity with God. We know about sin only in relation to Jesus' victory over sin in the cross and resurrection.

Humans live in misery because of sin. We have gone away from our home in God to live in the "far country" (as with the prodigal son in Luke 15). We prefer our own lives below rather than the divine life above. Humans are slothful, an expression of their pride in wanting to live for themselves instead of for God.

But Jesus has taken on our misery. Jesus, the Word of God, enters the world and lives as a human being, humbling himself and coming to us in our misery. Jesus took on our misery to himself as his own. Jesus knows the darkness of human misery. He knows it more than anyone else ever did since he took all human sin and misery upon himself on the cross.

Through the cross and passion of Jesus, we who are sinners are reconciled with God. As Barth put it, "we are all away from home—exiles. In Jesus we are all back home again." Human misery is left behind. Now we are freed from misery and "alive to God in Christ Jesus" (Rom 6:11). Now we are covenant partners with God, not covenant breakers. Now we "enter into the joy" (Matt 25:21, 23) living in union and communion with Jesus Christ. We are back home again!

2. Barth, *Church Dogmatics* IV/2, 488.

41

My Grace . . . for You

> My grace—that is *myself*: I for you, I as your Savior in your place—I who set you free from sin, guilt, misery, and death, all of which I have taken on myself and so away from you—I who show you the Father and open up the path to him—I who let you hear the great Yes which he spoke to you too, to you personally, from all eternity—I who in this way appoint and install you as God's servant and who make you useful, ready and willing for this particular service.[3]

++++

Our lives and ministries for Jesus Christ originate from God's grace. We do not choose God; God chooses us (John 15:16).

Barth spoke of "My grace is enough" (2 Cor 12:9) and hears these words today. God's grace "is *myself*"—God as our Savior in Jesus Christ gave us himself and "set you free from sin, guilt, misery, and death, all of which I have taken on myself and so away from you." This is Christ's grace of liberation and freedom.

Jesus shows us "the Father and open[s] up the path to him." "I," says Jesus, "let you hear the great Yes which he spoke to you too, to you personally, from all eternity." This is God's acceptance, God speaking "Yes" to us in Christ; God's gracious election of us to know God is for us in Christ.

Our election leads us to serve God. Christ says it is "I who in this way appoint and install you as God's servant and who make you useful, ready and willing for this particular service." We serve by God's grace. We serve God with our whole lives in response to "my grace . . . for you!"

3. Barth, *Call for God*, 83 (italics his).

42

In God We Have Every Blessing

> God has nothing higher than this to give, namely himself; because in giving us himself, he has given us every blessing.[4]

++++

Barth constantly speaks of God's love shown to us in Jesus Christ. This is the center of the "good news of great joy for all the people," (Luke 2:10) of which the angels sang at the birth of Jesus.

Today, we speak of the blessings God gives us throughout our lives in so many ways. No day goes by where we do not remember our blessings and give thanks to God for them. This is a rhythm in our lives: We are blessed by God; we praise and thank God for our blessings.

But the greatest blessing of all is Jesus Christ himself. As Barth put it: "God has nothing higher than this to give, namely himself; because in giving us himself, he has given us every blessing." God has given us God's own self in Jesus Christ, the eternal Son of God. Jesus has come to live among us, to die for the forgiveness of sins (Col 1:14), and was raised from the dead for our justification (Rom 4:25). Jesus Christ has done all this for us! God has given us God's own self in Jesus Christ, and in him God has "given us every blessing."

All the blessings of God we experience in our daily lives come from the one, single blessing—the greatest blessing of all: *God's own self given to us in Jesus Christ!* Christ is the singular blessing of God, the one blessing from whom all other blessings flow.

When we count our blessings—all the ways we daily experience God's blessings in our lives through his loving care and grace—we begin and end with the greatest blessing in which all other blessings originate: Jesus Christ!

4. Barth, *Church Dogmatics* II/1, 275.

43

God Holds Us

> The truth of Easter day, like the truth of Good Friday—is this, that God holds us fast, whoever we are and whatever our situation, whatever we may feel and think, however difficult our mood may be today and tomorrow, because, and by the very fact that, we have once again abandoned him and continually abandon him. He is present, he does not abandon us, even when we cannot help thinking ourselves abandoned. . . . The truth is that he is completely and utterly ours and that we may be completely and utterly his. That is the Easter message.[5]

++++

The great theological truths of the Christian faith have tremendous significance for our lives. In an Easter sermon (1961), Barth reminds us above that Good Friday and Easter mean "God holds us fast." No matter who we are or what our situation, in the most difficult times of life, God holds us. Even when we abandon God, as Christians, God does not abandon us. God holds us. This is the message we need for living.

Good Friday assures us that God is for us in Jesus' dying for our sins. Easter assures us God is with us since Jesus is risen and alive forevermore. Nothing can cut us off from God's continuing, holding power. Even when we fear and think God would not want to hold us, or that God will not hold us, God holds us! We do abandon God in our lives—going our own ways, sinning—even as Christians. But God is always present and will not abandon us. God is "completely and utterly ours." In response, "we may be completely and utterly" God's. Easter is every day. God holds us!

5. Barth, *Call for God*, 54–55.

44

Grace! Peace!

> Despite God's holiness, Grace! Despite human sin, Peace![6]

++++

The letter to the Ephesians begins with the greeting: "Grace to you and peace from God our Father and the Lord Jesus Christ" (Eph 1:2). This may sound like a typical, perfunctory greeting for a letter we might write: "I hope this finds you doing well . . . ." But this greeting is powerful. It speaks to the church at Ephesus, just as it speaks to us, today. It mentions two powerful words that are crucial to our experience as Christians: "grace" and "peace."

These important theological words speak to our lives as those who have received grace and peace in Jesus Christ. When he commented on this verse, Barth wrote: "Despite God's holiness, Grace! Despite human sin, Peace!" These show us what is at stake here.

God is holy. We are sinful. We deserve the judgment of God. But "despite God's holiness, Grace!" God gives grace—forgiving, healing, saving grace, giving us what we do not deserve; and not giving us what we do deserve. By grace we are saved; not by our own efforts or good works (Eph 2:8–9), but purely by God's good pleasure—God's grace to us in Jesus Christ.

We are sinners. But God gives peace. Jesus Christ has made "peace through the blood of his cross" (Col 1:20). This peace reestablishes the relationship God desires for us. We are justified by faith and have "peace with God through our Lord Jesus Christ" (Rom 5:1). This is "the peace of God, which surpasses all understanding" which keeps our hearts and minds in Christ Jesus (Phil 4:7). No other peace can do what the peace of God can do.

May God's grace and peace permeate our lives: "Despite God's holiness, Grace! Despite human sin, Peace!"

6. Barth, *Epistle to the Ephesians*, 77.

45

Baptism—Christ's Death Was Our Death

> Baptism is a representation of Christ's death in the midst of our life. It tells us that when Christ has been dead and buried we too have been dead and buried, we the transgressors and sinners. As one baptized you may see yourself as dead. The forgiveness of sins rests on the fact that this dying took place at that time on Golgotha. Baptism tells you that that death was also your death.[7]

++++

Baptism is significant in the church. It is significant in the life of the person baptized. Barth emphasized that baptism is an event about which we can think for our entire lives. He cites Luther, who said that when he was tempted he called to mind: "I have been baptized."[8]

Baptism is a signal. It points us to being witnesses and repenting of our sin. Baptism witnesses that we belong to God in Jesus Christ. Baptism, said Barth, is "a representation of Christ's death in the midst of our life. It tells us that when Christ has been dead and buried we too have been dead and buried, we the transgressors and sinners." As Paul wrote, "We have been buried with him by baptism into death" (Rom 6:4). We sinners have been baptized into Christ, so that now we can be "dead to sin and alive to God in Christ Jesus" (6:11).

In baptism, our sin is forgiven because Christ died for us "on Golgotha." Christ's death was for the whole world, including me. Jesus Christ stepped into the place of sinners. Christ reconciled us to God by taking responsibility for our sin so now we belong to him. Barth said, "Baptism tells you that that death was also your

7. Barth, *Dogmatics in Outline*, 151.

8. Luther, *Luther's Works* (Philadelphia), 54:86. Cf. McKim, *Moments with Martin Luther*, 97.

death." Christ does for us what we cannot do for ourselves. He carries our sin so we can be forgiven and receive new life.

46
Being Merry and Cheerful

> But we must also remember that the man who hears and takes to heart the biblical message is not only not permitted but plainly forbidden to be anything but merry and cheerful.[9]

++++

Many things that bring us joys and sorrows come and go. Life is a mixed bag, with happiness and sadness.

But overall, there is a deep pulsating joy that stands at the core of Christian life. The book of Nehemiah says, "the joy of the Lord is your strength" (Neh 8:10). The Psalms are full of references to joy, through and through. "My lips will shout for joy when I sing praises to you" (Ps 71:23) is one such verse. The letter to the Philippians is sometimes called "the epistle of joy."

What unites these verses and others is joy before the Lord because of the salvation, grace, and blessings God has given. Joy radiates outwardly from the deep sense of God's overwhelming, loving grace, which stands at the heart of the biblical message. As Barth put it: "We must also remember that the man who hears and takes to heart the biblical message is not only not permitted but plainly forbidden to be anything but merry and cheerful."

When we are grasped by the biblical message, we can be nothing but joyful people. We must be! Being "merry and cheerful" are expressions of the abiding message on which our lives in Jesus Christ are built. Succinctly: "Christ Jesus came into the world to save sinners" (1 Tim 1:15). The "good news of great joy" that the angels proclaimed at Jesus' birth is news of "a Savior, who is the Messiah, the Lord" (Luke 2:10, 11).

We are people of joy who are merry and cheerful: Jesus Christ is born!

9. Barth, *Church Dogmatics* III/4, 376.

47

Great Joy Cancels Fear

> The great joy—"To you is born this day a Savior"—was the negation of the great fear. But it was great joy only as the negation of the great fear, only as the cancellation of fear before God by the eternal mercy of God, and only as forgiveness granted to those who cannot justify themselves.[10]

++++

Fears abound for us on many sides. Some fears are more grave than others. Climate change, the threat of war, fears of a terminal illness—these get our attention because they can be so devastating and so real. Other fears may pale in comparison, but they are real nonetheless. The normal fears of the day-to-day can nag as well: financial security, raising a family, entering our later years. Worries, doubts, uncertainties all can be sources of fear for us.

Our greatest fear is our fear of death. Death is the great unknown. There is a natural fear before God which we fear we will encounter after our physical life is finished.

Barth proclaims the gospel message of "the great joy—'To you is born this day a Savior'" (Luke 2:11) as the way our greatest fear is negated. Our fear of death and fear of God are countered by this word of redemption and hope. This message is "the cancellation of fear before God by the eternal mercy of God." God's eternal mercy is the only hope and assurance to counter our fear of death and God's judgment on our sin. We need a Savior—Jesus Christ.

God's eternal mercy in Jesus grants forgiveness "to those who cannot justify themselves." Our fearfulness gives way to fearlessness. Fears great and small are gone. Great joy cancels fear! Receive this joy of our Savior!

10. Barth, *Christmas*, 33, from the 1929 Sermon, "Be Not Afraid."

48

With Thanksgiving

> To be anxious means that we ourselves suffer, ourselves groan, ourselves seek to see ahead. Thanksgiving means giving God the glory in everything, making room for him, casting our care on him, let it be his care. The troubles that exercise us then cease to be hidden and bottled up. They are so to speak laid open towards God, spread out before him.[11]

++++

If we read only the first words of Philippians 4:6, we wonder how Paul could be serious: "Do not worry [be anxious] about anything." Really? If there two things with which we are well acquainted, they are worry and anxiety. They rise with us in the morning and go to bed with us at night. What helps us?

We have to keep reading Paul's words: "But in everything by prayer and supplication with thanksgiving let your requests be made known to God" (Phil 4:6). The antidote to worry and anxiety is prayer—to ask for God's help, with thanksgiving!

As Barth explains, worry and anxiety are how we feel when we want to control the future. We suffer, groan, and try to anticipate what lies ahead. But Paul urges us to cast our anxieties and worries on God through prayer, our requests made "with thanksgiving."

We can entrust our futures to God with the thanksgiving that enables us to give God glory "in everything." Our view of the present and future can make room for God as we cast our cares on God and let those cares now become God's cares! Now our troubles are no longer hidden, they all hang out, spread out before God. God now shares our cares. What can help us more?!

11. Barth, *Epistle to the Philippians*, 122.

To turn over all to God—with thanksgiving!—this is the antidote to anxiety and worry. This brings peace (Phil 4:7), grounded in Jesus Christ. Let's live always: with thanksgiving!

49
Grace and Gratitude

> The only answer to χάρις (*charis*) is εὐχαριστία (*eucharistia*); . . . χάρις (*charis*) always demands the answer of εὐχαριστία. Grace and gratitude belong together like heaven and earth. Grace evokes gratitude like the voice an echo. Gratitude follows grace like thunder lightning.[12]

++++

We're all familiar with an echo. In the right place, a sound made is followed by a reflection of the sound—an echo. An echo happens in response to a sound; and it inevitably follows the sound. So it is, says Barth, with grace and gratitude.

Put in plain English, Barth wrote that the only answer to grace is gratitude. God's grace always demands the answer of gratitude. The Greek and Latin terms show the linguistic relationships here. See the roots in each of the terms: χάρις (*charis*) is "grace"; εὐχαριστία (*eucharistia*) is "gratitude." "χάρις" "grace" is in each term; *charis* is in each term. Linguistically, the terms are in the closest possible relationship. Theologically, the terms are in the closest possible relationship.

God's grace evokes our gratitude. We are grateful for the grace God gives. Barth uses images to show the interconnections: "Grace and gratitude belong together like heaven and earth. Grace evokes gratitude like the voice an echo. Gratitude follows grace like thunder lightning." Only our gratitude can correspond to God's grace. What God does in us and for us calls forth our deepest gratitude. There is nothing for which we should be more thankful; there is no other gift which can mean more for us than the gift of God's grace. Grace is God's free gift (Eph 2:8; 3:7) to which we can only respond by expressing the depths of our thankfulness and grateful praise!

12. Barth, *Church Dogmatics* IV/1, 41.

A voice and an echo; thunder and lightning—how well are we expressing our gratitude for the grace of God?

50
Joy and Gratitude

> Joy is really the simplest form of gratitude. . . . To be joyful is to look out for opportunities for gratitude.[13]

++++

The gratitude we feel as we receive the grace of God in our lives moves us in new directions. We are constantly amazed at what forms these new directions take. As grateful people, we express our gratitude in new and ever-changing ways.

But in gratitude one characteristic is always the same. As we experience and express gratitude, we have joy. Joy. Joy is that feeling of deepest delight that spills into happiness and a sense of contentment and gladness. Joy can make us feel that time stands still as we experience enjoyment that overflows.

Barth wrote that "joy is really the simplest form of gratitude." Joy is our primary reaction to receive God's grace in ways that make our hearts overflow with gratitude. We express our gratitude in many ways—but joy is always our companion!

Relatedly, Barth also wrote that "to be joyful is to look out for opportunities for gratitude." As we are joyful in the gratitude we find in God's grace, our joy will lead us to be on the lookout for opportunities to express more gratitude. As joyful people of God, we experience God's gift of grace in life and find fulfillment in the blessings God's gifts bring. When the Holy Spirit brings us God's joys we will look to find ways by which our gratitude can be expressed in more and more ways.

There is a kind of back-and-forth motion at work here. Gratitude brings joy; joy leads us to look for gratitude more and more. When gratitude and joy mark our lives, we realize God's Spirit is bringing us "grace upon grace" (John 1:16).

13. Barth, *Church Dogmatics* III/4, 376, 378.

51

Receiving from God and Active for God

> Because God is for us, we may also be for him. Because he has given himself to us, we may also in gratitude give him the trifle which we have to give. To hold to God thus always means that we receive everything wholly from God and so are wholly active for him.[14]

++++

Our relationship with God in Jesus Christ is total and comprehensive. The center of the gospel is that God loves us in Christ, forgiving our sin and reconciling us to God. In Jesus Christ we see that "God is for us." This is the good news we need to know! God is for us in Jesus Christ. Our response to this gospel message is that "we may also be for him."

These are the big moments in our lives, aren't they? They are moments that in one sense happen once and for all for us. We are reconciled to God in Christ; we are new creations in Christ and live as people of faith in service to God as disciples of Jesus Christ.

But these moments also occur for us over and over again. Daily we are aware that in Christ, "God is for us." Daily we stand at the foot of the cross and confess with the disciple Thomas: "My Lord and my God" (John 20:28)! Daily we, like the disciple Levi, respond to Jesus' call: "Follow me" (Mark 2:14). We receive from God and we are active for God—wholly!

Our response of obedience is an expression of gratitude for what God has given us. We give God, says Barth, "the trifle which we have to give." We give our whole lives in grateful service for the "indescribable gift" (2 Cor 9:15) we have in Christ!

14. Barth, *Dogmatics in Outline*, 19.

52

Knowledge of God Is Obedience to God

Knowledge of God is obedience to God.[15]

++++

Of all the knowledge we have in life, surely the most important is knowledge of God. What else could matter more? If there is a God with whom we deal, we need to know who God is, what God has done, and the nature of God. These are basic theological issues and many questions arise from them.

Barth strongly believed that for the Christian, the true knowledge of God comes when God is revealed, is made known to humans. We cannot know God by our own powers of reason, experience, or anything else. Barth rejected natural theology. If God is to be known, God must choose to be revealed.

The good news of Christian faith is that God is revealed! God is known in Jesus Christ, God's Son: "the Word became flesh and lived among us" (John 1:14). This is the knowledge of faith. It affirms that who God is becomes known by what God does. God is revealed in God's works.

When by faith we know the God who acts, we become obedient to God. As Barth wrote, "Knowledge of God is obedience to God." Since God is the one who acts, as we see in Scripture and supremely in Jesus Christ, we must be engaged with God. We cannot treat God like a mathematical formula or keep God as an object of knowledge, an intellectual concept. Because God acts, we must obey! We are involved with God—the God who is involved with us.

15. Barth, *Church Dogmatics* II/1, 26.

Each day we need to realize the God we know in Jesus Christ is the God we obey. We do not look at God; we live with God! To know God is to obey God. As Paul said, "In him we live and move and have our being" (Acts 17:28).

53
Make God's Purposes Our Desire

> [God] does not will to be God without us, or to exist as such. He calls us to his side. He summons us to make his purposes and aims the object of our own desire. Hence he takes no account of our godlessness. He reckons us among his own.[16]

++++

Jesus invited his disciples to pray and gave us the Lord's Prayer as a model prayer for our own. Today, we may take the Lord's Prayer for granted. Its words are so familiar. But the prayer is deeply rich and each phrase should be meditated upon fully.

By inviting his disciples to pray, Jesus was saying, as Barth puts it, that God "does not will to be God without us, or to exist as such." God shares God's life with us. God "calls us" to God's side, summoning us to make God's purposes and aims our desire. This is an astounding recognition: God can do whatever God wants in this world. God does not need human help. But in prayer, God cuts us in on the action and invites us to make God's purposes our purposes, God's desires our desires.

In the first three petitions of the Lord's Prayer—"hallowed be thy name," "thy kingdom come," "thy will be done"—God invites us to take up God's cause and participate in it by our asking. God is calling us to God's side to make God's purposes our desire. Despite our godlessness—our sinfulness—even as God's people, God takes "no account," says Barth, and "reckons us among his own." We pray for God's purposes; and work for God's purposes since God "does not will to be God without us." Amazing!

What greater blessing than to participate with God in doing God's work. In prayer we make God's purposes our desire!

16. Barth, *Church Dogmatics* III/4, 104.

54

The Great Passion

> [Hallowed be thy name]
>
> Christians are people with a definite passion. In no circumstances, then, can they be cowards, blind-worms, bored, boring, or commonplace. . . . The distinctive Christian passion[:] Its concern is for the honor of God. . . . The Christian thinks and speaks and acts with this desire when he seriously prays the first petition. He is filled, impelled, guided, and ruled by this hot desire.[17]

++++

We tend to think that passionate Christians are an exception. They may be overzealous in our view, making too much of a show, or wearing their faith on their sleeve, as the saying goes.

But Barth emphasized that "Christians are people with a definite passion. In no circumstances, then, can they be cowards, blind-worms, bored, boring, or commonplace." If our faith means more to us than anything else, then our faith should show itself. We are not to blend in with our culture. We are to be people of passion, expressing our faith in Jesus Christ.

What is our passion? Barth said the Christian's "distinctive Christian passion" is "concern . . . for the honor of God." In explaining the first petition of the Lord's Prayer, "Hallowed by thy name," Barth urged that we be "filled, impelled, guided, and ruled by this hot desire." Zeal for the honor of God is characteristic of people such as Elijah, Paul, and Peter. The hallowing of God's name is the passionate desire for God's name to be known and loved through all the earth. This has not happened yet, so the Christian continues to pray this petition in the Lord's Prayer.

17. Barth, *Christian Life*, 111, 113.

Those who are not Christians do not care or pray for God's name to be honored. If we lose this zeal for the honor of God, we can no longer be a Christian. What are we doing to express our great passion: zeal for the honor of God?

55

The Creatures God Loves

> The man with whom we have to do in ourselves and in others, although a rebel, a sluggard, a hypocrite, is likewise the creature to whom his Creator is faithful and not unfaithful. But there is still more: he is the being whom God has loved, loves, and will love because he has substituted himself in Jesus Christ and made himself the guarantee.[18]

++++

Humans are sinners and sin is to be taken with great seriousness. Barth wrote much about this, emphasizing that humans are "not good," we are covenant breakers, and that God's speaks a "No" to human sin.

But Jesus Christ has taken upon himself this "No" of sin. Jesus takes our sin upon himself through his death on the cross. Jesus has died so the "No" will no longer affect us. Jesus Christ is God's "Yes" to humanity. As Paul put it: "God proves his love for us in that while we still were sinners Christ died for us" (Rom 5:8).

Barth emphasized that a human who is "a rebel, a sluggard, a hypocrite," is "likewise the creature to whom his Creator is faithful and not unfaithful." God does not turn away from us—sinners that we are. God continues in faithfulness to seek and save the lost (see Luke 19:10).

But there is even more, said Barth. The sinner is "the being whom God has loved, loves, and will love because he has substituted himself in Jesus Christ and made himself the guarantee." God's love for sinners is constant. It is deep and profound: "For God so loved the world that he gave his only Son" (John 3:16). Jesus Christ made himself the guarantee that we are creatures God loves!

18. Barth, *Humanity of God*, 60.

56

Christ Concealed in the Neighbor

Jesus Christ is always concealed in the neighbor.[19]

++++

We exist in two relationships. Jesus said the two great commandments are to love God and love our neighbors (Mark 12:28–31). One relationship is with the invisible God. The other is with the visible neighbor. Our lives are to be lived and fulfilled in the rhythm of these two loves.

In his incarnation, Jesus Christ has made himself our neighbor. In his resurrection, Christ has revealed himself as our neighbor according to Barth. This unites us with all other persons. Christ is neighbor to us all. Distant or nearby, our neighbor is one we are to love. We allow neighbors to serve us and we witness to neighbors of God's loving presence with us in Jesus Christ.

This leads Barth to say that "Jesus Christ is always concealed in the neighbor." The neighbor is not a second revelation of Christ or a second Christ, but in the neighbor whom we are to love, we perceive Jesus Christ himself, who is our neighbor. We will speak to our neighbor of Jesus Christ. This is an expression of genuine love for a neighbor. If there is genuine love, the name of Jesus cannot be withheld.

Our witness of love to neighbors means we assist our neighbor as a sign of the promised help of God. Our witness is to Jesus Christ, who is Helper in life and in life beyond death.

Our witness is in word and deed. We must always be ready to act for our neighbor. We seek to help relieve needs and provide assistance. We are to be ready for service in what we say and what we do.

19. Barth, *Church Dogmatics* I/2, 435. Cf. I/2, 424, 434.

Will we see Jesus Christ concealed in our neighbor? Will we love our neighbor, as we are loved in our true neighbor, Jesus Christ himself?

57

Jesus Is the Good Samaritan

> In the true sense he [Jesus] is the Samaritan who in Lk 10:25f. does not, like the priest and the Levite, pass by on the other side, when he comes on the man who had fallen among thieves and was left half-dead by the roadside, but shows mercy on him, thus acting as, and proving himself to be, the neighbor of the lawyer's question. In the true sense it is he who fulfills the commandments of Deut 6:4 and Lev 19:18. In the true sense it is he who performs the act of love in both its dimensions.[20]

++++

Jesus told the parable of the good Samaritan (Luke 10:25–37) in response to the question of a lawyer: "'What must I do to inherit eternal life?'" Jesus asked what the law thought. The lawyer responded, "'You shall love the Lord your God with all your heart, and with all your soul, and with all your strength, and with all your mind; and your neighbor as yourself'" (see Deut 6:4; Lev 19:18). Jesus said, "'Do this, and you will live.' But the lawyer asked Jesus, "'And who is my neighbor?'" This led to Jesus' parable.

Barth interpreted this parable to say the neighbor is the one who shows compassion. In this sense, the Samaritan, who was "a neighbor to the man who fell into the hands of the robbers" (Luke 10:36), became one who conveyed and represented the divine compassion of God to the person in great need. Unlike the priest and Levite, who passed by, the Samaritan showed mercy on the man half-dead by the roadside.

Jesus Christ is the good Samaritan. He is the true neighbor, who loved God and loved a neighbor in need. In this, Jesus fulfilled the law. Do we hear Jesus saying to us: "Go and do likewise?"

20. Barth, *Church Dogmatics* IV/2, 823. Cf. I/2, 410–50.

58

Love Always

> The Christian life begins with love. It also ends with love, so far as it has an end as human life in time.[21]

++++

Love is central to Christian faith. Love is the essence of God (1 John 4:16). "Whoever does not love does not know God, for God is love" (1 John 4:8).

Barth stressed the comprehensive nature of love when he wrote that "the Christian life begins with love. It also ends with love, so far as it has an end as human life in time." In the beginning and ending of our Christian lives, love is central. Barth also went on to say that "love is the essence of Christian living."[22] Throughout our lives as Christian persons, to love is our dominant verb. Love always!

Our faith in Jesus Christ leads us to love. We know the nature of God's true love for us through Jesus Christ. As Paul put it, "God proves his love for us in that while we still were sinners Christ died for us" (Rom 5:8). When we come to faith, we begin to love. Love expresses our faith. "If we did not begin to love," wrote Barth, "we would not have come to faith."[23] Faith expresses itself in love of God and love of neighbor. In Jesus' parable of the last judgment, it is those who love and serve people in need who find themselves blessed (Matt 25:31–46).

A gospel chorus proclaims: "Love, love, love, love, the gospel in a word is love." The measure of our lives in Christ is the love we show. As someone said, "love is something you *do*." Barth put it

21. Barth, *Church Dogmatics* I/2, 371.
22. Barth, *Church Dogmatics*, I/2, 372.
23. Barth, *Church Dogmatics* I/2, 371.

bluntly: "In eternity when we see God face to face, either we will be those who love, or we will not be."[24] Do we love?

24. Barth, *Church Dogmatics* I/2, 372.

59

Look on Jesus Christ

> We must not seek to know about God or man except as we look on Jesus Christ.[25]

++++

God is the electing God who acts for humanity in Jesus Christ. Jesus Christ is the Word of God in whom the fullness of God dwells and who is a unity of true divinity and true humanity. This is a statement of Christology, of who Jesus Christ is. The work of Jesus Christ is his work of salvation. In Christ's life, death, resurrection, and ascension, God has acted to bring salvation to the world through Jesus Christ.

It is through Jesus Christ that we know God. As Barth put it, "we must not seek to know about God or man except as we look on Jesus Christ." For Barth, Christology is the center of all theology because our knowledge of God comes through our knowledge of Jesus Christ. There is no other path or route to true knowledge of the God we find revealed in the Scriptures.

This means that God's will is revealed in Jesus Christ. When we want to know what God has done or what God wants us to do, we look at Jesus Christ. Since Jesus is "God with us," his words and teachings are guides for our lives. Jesus honored the Old Testament law; and saw the law as fulfilled in his own life and work (Luke 24:44). His death carried out God's will as the means for providing salvation. We look on Jesus Christ to know what God desires.

Most practically, this means that Jesus is the norm for our living. We see in his life—his forgiving love, his desire for peace and justice, his call to discipleship—the directions in which God wants us to live and move. Look on Jesus Christ!

25. Barth, *Church Dogmatics* II/2, 150.

60

Regard All as Those for Whom Christ Died

> Their decisive presupposition in respect of every man can be only that Jesus Christ has died for his sin too, and for his salvation. They must regard and approach every man from this angle. Hence they can never be against men. They can only be for them, not just theoretically but practically, with their action or inaction, their speech or silence, their intervention or toleration, as these procure space and courage and joy for them simply as men.[26]

++++

Martin Luther said the Christian is at the same time "justified and a sinner."[27] We are justified by faith as we believe Jesus Christ died for us. Yet we also continue to sin, even as Christians.

If God loves us—such as we are—then, said Barth, we should look on others this way as well. The one decisive thing we should recognize in respect to every person we meet can only be that Jesus Christ has died for that person's sin too, and for that person's salvation. As Christians, we look at every person from this angle. This is the one, most important fact about all people: Jesus Christ died for them.

This means, said Barth, that we "can never be against" other people. We can "only be for them, not just theoretically but practically." As God is for us, in Jesus Christ, we are to be for others. Not only must we believe this truth; we must also live this truth. Whatever the "action or inaction" of others, "their speech or silence, their intervention or toleration, as these procure space and courage and joy for them" we are for them simply as persons.

26. Barth, *Church Dogmatics*, III/4, 503–4.

27. Luther, *Luther's Works* (St. Louis), 25:260. Cf. McKim, *Moments with Martin Luther*, 26.

We regard all persons as those for whom Jesus Christ died. No matter who they are or what they do, this is what means the most. Let's live it!

61

Accept the Word of Reconciliation

> To know Jesus Christ is to accept the Word of reconciliation spoken in him and his prophetic work. It is thus to accept a Word which is new and strange to the world reconciled in him.[28]

++++

Sometimes people think it is easy to be a Christian. Just believe in Jesus and you are all set. It's an easy thing to say, so being a Christian can be simple and trouble-free—especially in a culture where Christians are dominant.

But Barth says that on the contrary, living as a Christian means one is aware of burdens laid on us that other people do not have to bear. We know we are inescapably in solidarity with all persons and indeed, with all creatures, in the sorrows that befall all creatures. We know the difficulties of the tasks God sets before us as disciples of Jesus Christ. Our efforts for the gospel of Christ may be thankless and, from a human point of view, unsuccessful.

Most of all, as Barth writes, "To know Jesus Christ is to accept the Word of reconciliation spoken in him and his prophetic work. It is thus to accept a Word which is new and strange to the world reconciled in him." We accept reconciliation in Christ when the world itself opposes Christ by what it thinks and says and practices. This is constant opposition, at every turn. We have to face it.

To accept the word of reconciliation of the world in Jesus Christ means, says Barth, that we "take the side of Jesus Christ" and take responsibility for the cause of Christ, rather than being passive spectators. Christ's work is what we try to do in a world where the word of reconciliation is "new and strange." We hear Christ's word and seek to live it!

28. Barth, *Church Dogmatics* IV/3/1, 366.

62

Prayer Replaces Anxiety

> Shall we be alive tomorrow? Prayer must take the place of anxiety and form the basis of work for the morrow. The children of God are not anxious about work. They work because they pray.[29]

++++

Anxiety is a fact of life. We often find ourselves anxious about many things. These anxieties range from big issues—such as "Shall we be alive tomorrow?"—to smaller ones—"What shall I wear to the meeting tomorrow?" Anxiety causes us to fret and worry. No matter how much we try, we cannot be rid of anxiety.

If we take this big issue of life, which Barth mentions—"Shall we be alive tomorrow?"—we find the only antidote for anxiety is prayer. This is what Barth suggested: "Prayer must take the place of anxiety and form the basis of work for the morrow." Instead of worrying and being anxious about our lives and what tomorrow may or may not bring, our only hope and help is to entrust ourselves fully to God, through prayer. Our life and work tomorrow cannot be based on what we can control because so much is beyond our control. Instead, we should entrust ourselves—our lives and work—to God. In prayer, we can trust that our work tomorrow is in God's hands. By giving over all things to God in prayer, our work will proceed as we live the lives God gives us—today and tomorrow.

In short, Barth says that "the children of God are not anxious about work. They work because they pray." All we are and do is given by God. In prayer, we recognize our dependence on God. We trust God. We receive the good gifts God gives—including our work—and live prayerful lives in faith and hope.

29. Barth, *Prayer*, 50.

63

The Miracle of the Mercy of God

> The Christian life . . . is constituted by the miracle of the mercy of God.[30]

++++

We are most thankful in our lives for times we have received mercy. If we have done something for which we rightly deserve retribution, punishment, or payback—justice is deserved; and if we receive mercy instead, the depths of our gratitude know no bounds.

So we understand what Barth meant when wrote that "The Christian life . . . is constituted by the miracle of the mercy of God." We are Christians today because of the miracle of the mercy of God.

In the biblical story, humans sin against God and deserve death because of this disobedience. This is our human lot. This is our own personal story. We do not deserve or merit God's favor or love. We face judgment for our actions.

But Barth spoke of us being "inconceivably upheld over the abyss of the death to which we have fallen victim and which we have merited."[31] We have been "like a brand snatched from the fire" as Amos said (Amos 4:11). Inconceivably, instead of receiving what we deserve—judgment and justice—we receive "the miracle of the mercy of God."

The name of this mercy is Jesus Christ. In Christ, God has taken up our cause and come to our assistance. God enters into our distress and takes on our sin by suffering and dying in our place in Jesus' death on the cross.

30. Barth, *Ethics*, 403.

31. Barth, *Ethics*, 404.

For Barth, "that our deeds should bear witness to this is what is required of us."[32] We witness to Christ as the one who has snatched us from the fire we deserve and mercifully reconciled us to God through forgiveness of our sin. Now we know we are not our own, but God's. God's goodness and patience daily point us to Christ, who covers and bears our sin.

Be thankful for "the miracle of God's mercy" every day!

32. Barth, *Ethics*, 404.

64

Humility: Trust in Despair

> Humility is courage. It is the attitude of those who are held up in their fall and saved in their lostness. It is not despair but trust in despair.[33]

++++

Sometimes humility is criticized as a virtue. In the tradition of Aristotelian ethics, humility was seen as a roadblock to greatness. Some modern philosophers see humility as leading to unhappiness and human degradation.

But humility in the Scriptures is the attitude of the sinner who is upheld by God's grace and mercy. It is our right response to God's love, which seeks out sinners in Jesus Christ, who has reconciled us to God and drawn us to himself. Christ stands in for us and gives us himself.

We live by this consciousness of what God has done in Jesus Christ. We will always be living in lowliness before God. But as Barth put it, "Humility is courage. It is the attitude of those who are held up in their fall and saved in their lostness. It is not despair but trust in despair." True courage comes from recognizing our situation and trusting God in Christ in the midst of the despair of our sinful situations. We are "held up" in our fall and "saved in our lostness."

The Scriptures say, "'God opposes the proud, but gives grace to the humble'" (1 Pet 5:5; Jas 4:6). God gives grace. We can "walk humbly" with our God (see Mic 6:8) by trusting the God who saves us from despair and lostness and gives us courage. True humility is strength under control—not our own strength—but the strength of recognizing who we are and who, in humility, God enables us to be in Christ.

33. Barth, *Ethics*, 402.

Humility enables us to trust God in the midst of all the despairs of life since our greatest despair—our sin—has been forgiven in Christ.

65

Call Upon Me

> We thus understand the command, "Call upon me" (Ps 50:15), to be the basic meaning of every divine command, and we regard invocation according to this command as the basic meaning of all human obedience. What God permits man, what he expects, wills, and requires of him, is a life of calling upon him. This life of calling upon God will be a person's Christian life: his life in freedom, conversion, faith, gratitude, and faithfulness.[34]

++++

In Psalm 50:15, the psalmist wrote: "Call on me in the day of trouble; I will deliver you, and you shall glorify me." The verse seems much like a number of other verses in Psalms, so we may be tempted to overlook it.

But Barth saw this as a highly significant command of God. It is "the basic meaning of every divine command, and we regard invocation according to this command as the basic meaning of all human obedience." All God's commands point to this one. Calling on God in prayers is "the basic meaning of all human obedience." What other command could be more important than this?

Our lives are spent calling on God in prayer. This constitutes our Christian life. We have freedom to pray. We turn to God—our conversion. We call on God in faith, in trust. We call on God when we give God gratitude for God's grace. We pray for God's faithfulness to see us through all the times we have been unfaithful. In days of trouble and all situations, God says: "Call upon me."

Then we hear God's most wonderful promise and respond to God's command: "I will deliver you, and you shall glorify me." God wants us to call on God; and blesses us when we do!

34. Barth, *Christian Life*, 44. Cf. 89. Barth, *Church Dogmatics* III/3, 268. Cf. Barth, *Prayer*, 79.

LIVING AS A CHRISTIAN

66

One Long Calling Upon God

> [The Christian] life is positive in the fact that from the very first it is one long calling upon God. He calls upon God representatively for those who do not yet do so, or do not seem to do so. He does not exclude but includes them when he prays to this God: [Lord's Prayer]. This God will not faint, neither be weary. He hears all those who call on him in this way [Isa 40:28f.].[35]

++++

We are set on our Christian lives by Jesus Christ. Jesus bore his cross to Golgotha and died for our sins. We are set on a "glorious way," says Barth, by the resurrection of Jesus Christ. Our lives are difficult with the afflictions we bear. But they are also glorious since we live by the power of the resurrected Christ.

To live in this dialectic or tension we need God's help. Barth says our lives in Christ are positive since they are "one long calling upon God." We call on God in prayer—in times of affliction and in praise—for the presence of God in Christ among us through the Holy Spirit.

Our lives are "one long calling upon God" not only for ourselves, but for others, too. We pray to God for those who do not yet know God, or who seem not to know God. We include them as we pray all the petitions of the Lord's Prayer. Barth assures us "this God will not faint, neither be weary." God hears all who call on God throughout our whole lives. Barth quotes from Isaiah: "those who wait for the Lord shall renew their strength, they shall mount up with wings like eagles, they shall run and not be weary, they shall walk and not faint" (Isa 40:31).

Call upon God!

35. Barth, *Church Dogmatics* IV/3/1, 367.

67

In Prayer All Masks Fall

> In prayer—and this is why it is commanded—all masks and camouflages may and must fall away.[36]

++++

We realize people hide behind masks—even us. Masks are ways of speaking or acting that hide our true views or feelings, ways through which we hide our true selves. We function in society, with others, by adopting a persona, or a way we want others to perceive us. But deep down, we know this is not who we truly are. There is more, something different, or a core of ourselves we can never let others see.

In prayer, we come before God. We come before God as who we truly are. We address God with our petitions, our requests. In prayer, we can be our true selves; in fact, we must be our true selves. In our daily lives, we do what we may do—even helping and supporting others. But in prayer, we cannot do anything before God. We can only be before God. The masks we adopt—many even being necessary for doing what we do—these masks must come off before God. Barth wrote: "In prayer—and this is why it is commanded—all masks and camouflages may and must fall away."

We must be our true selves before God, not presenting God with all we do or have done. We come before the Lord with empty hands. God wills to fill our empty hands. We stand honestly before God in true trust and humility, not pretending to be who we are not, not covering our sins or failures, but opening ourselves completely to the one who knows us fully and most deeply.

To come before God with no pretenses can liberate us. We entrust our true selves to the God who hears our prayers—wearing no masks!

36. Barth, *Church Dogmatics* III/4, 98.

68
Asking

> It is an asking, a seeking, and a knocking directed toward God: a wishing a desiring and a requesting presented to God. . . . Prayer, or praying, is simply asking.[37]

++++

We recognize different dimensions or kinds of prayer. We recognize prayer as an element of worship—prayers of praise and thanksgiving to God happen in worship. We recognize prayer as prayers of confession and penitence, when we ask God's forgiveness for our sins.

Then there is prayer as petition. Barth discussed the first two types of prayer and argued that while prayer is rightly praise and penitence, first and foremost prayer is petition. Barth wrote: "It is an asking, a seeking, and a knocking directed toward God: a wishing, a desiring, and a requesting presented to God. . . . Prayer, or praying, is simply asking."

Barth appealed to the Lord's Prayer as proof. The model prayer Jesus taught his disciples is "clearly and simply a string of petitions, pure petitions . . . simply petition." This is the essence of prayer.

Prayer is simply asking. What a blessing! We can be bold to petition God, to ask God for the kinds of things the Lord's Prayer points us toward: the hallowing of God's name, the coming of God's reign, the doing of God's will, our daily bread, forgiveness, safety in temptation, deliverance from evil. These are the great needs Christians have. We do not take them for granted. In freedom, we petition and mightily ask God for these wishes and desires. Jesus himself commanded us to pray like this (Matt 6:9).

37. Barth, *Church Dogmatics* III/3, 268.

No prayer is too small or insignificant to bring to God. We seek help for our needs, for the needs of others, for the world's well-being. All these are big in the heart of God. So we pray and let our requests "be made known to God" (Phil 4:6).

69
Empty Hands

> Empty hands are necessary when human hands are to be spread out before God and filled by him. It is these empty hands that God in his goodness wills of us when he bids us pray to him.[38]

++++

The essence of prayer is petition, said Barth. God commands us to ask!

But it's important to recognize what our attitude should be as we pray and make our petitions to God.

Some may petition God believing they have a right to what they are asking for from the Lord. They may feel God owes it to them, or that they are worthy of receiving their requests. But this cannot be the case. What we receive from God, we receive not on the basis of our deserving, but by God's pure grace.

So Barth wrote that "empty hands are necessary when human hands are to be spread out before God and filled by him. It is these empty hands that God in his goodness wills of us when he bids us pray to him." As obedient children of God, we begin at the beginning each time we pray to God—nothing in our hands we bring.

We petition God realizing God alone is the Source of all good. We are completely dependent upon the Lord. We stand as needy people in relation to God. We are people of the covenant, joyfully coming before God and bringing nothing but ourselves as God's obedient people. We receive all things from God, by God's grace, and we receive God's blessings with open hands, claiming nothing for ourselves.

To pray to God with empty hands means we acknowledge God is the one who calls us into this covenant relationship. God

38. Barth, *Church Dogmatics* III/4, 97.

blesses our lives with what we need. Our greatest need is God; and into our empty hands, God gives us God's own self, in Jesus Christ!

70
The Perception of Grace Is Grace

> Grace is inaccessible to us: how else can it be grace? Grace can only make itself accessible. Grace can never be recalled. To remember grace is itself the work of grace. The perception of grace is itself grace.[39]

++++

Barth always emphasized that apart from Jesus Christ, we can know nothing about God and humanity and their relationship with each other. We ourselves cannot discover that God has entered into a covenant of grace with humanity in Jesus Christ and all this means for the new life of faith and obedience humans may experience. We know this only by God's grace.

Barth says "grace is inaccessible to us: how else can it be grace? Grace can only make itself accessible." We do not discover God's grace by our own efforts. If so, it would not be grace—it would be something we attain by our own powers or something we remember on our own. Only God's grace can bring God's grace to us.

Yet when we experience God's grace in Christ, Barth says, "to remember grace is itself the work of grace. The perception of grace is itself grace." This is a great blessing to be able to remember God's grace—that is another act of God's grace—a gift given to us! "The perception of grace is itself grace" means when we experience grace in our lives, when we recognize grace or recall it later, this recognition of the grace is itself yet more grace!

This makes the world come alive for us! Even our memories of God's grace to us—in Christ, in other people, in events—are new causes of thankfulness, remembering what God has done. So the whole world and all our relationships can abound with these pointers to God's grace to us—and supremely, to God's greatest grace in Jesus Christ!

39. Barth, *Church Dogmatics* IV/1, 45.

71

Our Ministry

> Our ministry is based upon the fact that we have been shown mercy. Jesus Christ has exercised his great patience toward us. Our service rests in the fact that we are thankful with a thankfulness which does not think of any reward, nor pride itself on any merit of its own. . . . Jesus Christ himself makes us servants. He does it solely through his caring to save sinners.[40]

++++

One way to describe our ministries as Christians is to say we are ministers of mercy. We share the mercy of God in Jesus Christ with others.

We can step back and also say we are ministers who have been shown mercy. The mercy we share is the mercy we have received in Christ. As Barth put it, "Our ministry is based upon the fact that we have been shown mercy. Jesus Christ has exercised his great patience toward us." We share mercy because we have received mercy.

We respond to the mercy we have received in Christ by being thankful. Our gratitude and thankfulness is based not on how deserving we are. Mercy is God's pure grace, given to us as unworthy sinners. We have no merit to claim or on which to rely. We do not seek reward, we simply receive mercy making us thankful from the depths of our hearts.

Our thankfulness leads us into the service of Jesus Christ. We give back the lives we owe. We are his disciples, followers who serve the world for which Christ died and to which Christ gives mercy. Barth wrote that "Jesus Christ himself makes us servants. He does it solely through his caring to save sinners." We are "servants of Christ" (1 Cor 4:1), thankful ministers of mercy!

40. Barth, *God in Action*, 68, 69.

72

Mission—Expanding the Truth of Christ

> Mission is objectively the expansion of the reality and truth of Jesus Christ. . . . Mission is concretely the going forth of salvation and its manifestation beyond the confines of Israel to the nations; the step in which the Messiah of Israel shows himself to be the Savior of the world.[41]

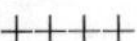

The Christian church has always been involved in mission. This has been defined in different ways, but it has involved the church's proclamation of Jesus Christ who calls disciples; the summons to conversion—our lives being turned in the direction of loving and serving God; and our being led into and living in the way of Jesus Christ. These actions occur in the name of the triune God: Father, Son, and Holy Spirit.

Most basically, mission is, as Barth said, "the expansion of the reality and truth of Jesus Christ." In whatever ways the church and Christian persons proclaim Jesus Christ in word and deeds, God's mission in this world is served (Latin, *missio Dei*).

The world is where the gospel of Christ is shared. Jesus said, "Go therefore and make disciples of all nations" (Matt 28:19). The truth of Christ expands through all the earth. As Barth put it, "Mission is concretely the going forth of salvation and its manifestation beyond the confines of Israel to the nations; the step in which the Messiah of Israel shows himself to be the Savior of the world."

To put it in the language of Jesus in the Gospel of John: "I am the Bread of Life" (John 6:35, 48), "for the Bread of God is that which comes down from heaven and gives life to the world"

41. Barth, *Church Dogmatics* IV/4, 97. Cf. IV/4, 96.

(John 6:33). The Messiah of Israel, the Bread of Life, gives life to the world by being the Savior of the world. Receive and proclaim the truth of Christ!

73

I Am a Witness to Jesus Christ

> The Christian is a witness, a witness of the living Jesus Christ as the Word of God and therefore a witness to the whole world and to all men of the divine act of grace which has taken place for all men. Thus in what makes him a Christian the first concern is not with his own person. He is referred, not to himself, but to God who points him to his neighbor, and to his neighbor who points him to God.[42]

++++

One thing that is true of us every day as Christian persons is that we are witnesses. Each believer, wrote Barth, is "a witness of the living Jesus Christ as the Word of God." This is a primary vocation or calling to us, that we are always to point beyond ourselves to Jesus Christ. Christ came for the world, and the Christian is "a witness to the whole world" and to all persons. We point to Christ as this unique and supreme "act of grace" given for every person. We receive God's gracious gift and proclaim Christ!

Barth always steers us away from self-focus, from looking first to ourselves. Instead, we look first and foremost to God and what God has done. What God has done for the world is what counts most. This is the Christian impulse, to look to God. When we do, we see God has acted in grace in Jesus Christ. In Christ, God points us to our neighbors. We are to love and serve them as Jesus Christ did. We live for others because we live for Christ.

Then we find that as we are pointed to our neighbors, our neighbors point us to God. In our neighbor, we see one for whom Christ died. We see all persons this way. So be who you are: a witness to Jesus Christ!

42. Barth, *Church Dogmatics* IV/3/2, 652.

74

The Church Exists for the World

> The true community of Jesus Christ is the community which God has sent out into the world in and with its foundation. As such it exists for the world.[43]

++++

Some see the church as a place of refuge, a place of retreat from the dangers and difficulties of the world in which we live. It can be appealing to close the door of the church building and wall it off from the society in which we live and the culture to which we relate.

But the true community of Jesus Christ—the church—exists for the world. The church community exists for God, and God exists for the world. The church does not exist for itself. It exists to be the people of God who witness to God's loving grace in Jesus Christ in the midst of the world where we are set. Looking at the world as Christian church members, we do not see the world in itself. We see the world centered as the focus of God's loving actions in Jesus Christ. In Christ, God is for the world.

So Barth wrote that "the true community of Jesus Christ is the community which God has sent out into the world in and with its foundation. As such it exists for the world." God sends us into the world, as witnesses to Jesus Christ, directed to the world, and as a community willing to give itself for others, as Jesus gave himself for us (Titus 2:14).

When we recognize this is the true vocation or calling of the church community, we will see the church as an ever-active, ever-giving, and ever-caring community, serving God by serving all persons in the world. The church does not exempt us from being in the world; it propels us into the world on behalf of the good news of Jesus Christ!

43. Barth, *Church Dogmatics* IV/3/2, 768.

75

The Community is Summoned to Action

> The community of Jesus Christ and the men united in it are bound to the world and everywhere summoned to action in relation to it. For God's active intervention for man, his eternal election of all men in the one, his giving of this one for all, his Word which goes out to all in this one, is the basis of its own being and existence.[44]

++++

The church of Jesus Christ is bound to Jesus Christ, our Lord. He is the great "head of the church" (Eph 5:23), the one who is the unity of the body of Christ.

The church is bound to Christ. But it is also bound to the world. Our lives in Christ are lives lived in the world and, says Barth, we are "everywhere summoned to action in relation to it." The world in which we live day by day as the community of Jesus Christ—the church—is where our lives in Christ take shape. The world around us is where we act, as the community of Christ, in faith—for the sake of the world.

This action is not just activism—action for the sake of action. We act here because God has actively intervened in the world—the world of sin—on behalf of all humanity. God has elected all persons in "this one"—Jesus Christ—whom God has given "for all."

The church's basis for being and its ground of existence is God's word "which goes out to all in this one." The church's one foundation is Jesus Christ—our Lord. The community lives in the world, the world that God loves, and for which Jesus Christ died (John 3:16).

44. Barth, *Church Dogmatics*, IV/3/2, 777.

The church community is summoned to action—on behalf of Jesus Christ. We are bound to the world as we are bound to our Lord and Savior.

76

Zeal for the Honor of God

> What is demanded of us Christians is no more and no less than zeal for the honor of God. . . . Those who look back to the first revelation of the hallowing of God's name that took place in Jesus Christ, and who also look forward to its second and final revelation, cannot come to terms and be satisfied with the status quo.[45]

++++

When we pray the Lord's Prayer, we may gloss over the first petition of the prayer: "Hallowed by your name" (Matt 6:9). But the implications of this petition are many!

Barth says that Christians who pray this prayer in obedience to Jesus' command are praying for "zeal for the honor of God." This is the "great passion" of Christians (see devotion #54).

We look back to "the first revelation of the hallowing of God's name" that "took place in Jesus Christ." God has acted in Jesus Christ, who has shown God's will and God's way for the world. We look forward to "its second and final revelation." Jesus will come again; the kingdom of God, which Jesus Christ himself was, will come in all its fullness.

An implication of praying this petition and having zeal for the honor of God is we "cannot come to terms and be satisfied with the status quo." In this "time between the times," between Jesus' first and second comings, our society and culture will exhibit the characteristics of a fallen, sinful world. Human actions will express the sinfulness of those who carry them out. The societal status quo will never be obedient to God's desires for the human community.

Christians pray and act for God's will and purposes for the world as we know them in Jesus Christ. Our passionate zeal is that God's name be honored in the midst of a sinful status quo.

45. Barth, *Christian Life*, 173.

77

Working for Peace

> The ministry of reconciliation also commits us to work honestly and earnestly for peace among the nations. In view of the means of mass destruction war is less than ever a possible solution of political and ideological tension between nations and power blocs.[46]

++++

God is a God of peace who has made peace and reconciled the world through the crucified and risen Jesus Christ. Christ announces a new humanity where hostilities between persons and nations are abolished. This is why Christians practice a "ministry of reconciliation" in this world (2 Cor 5:12–18).

Reconciliation is bringing people together in peace, overcoming the enmities that separate them. God's people work for reconciliation and peace in the world because this is what God desires and has established in Jesus Christ. Hatred and violence go against God's will, so Christians work for peace and reconciliation.

Working for peace is not an option for the Christian; it is an absolute necessity based on God's reconciling actions in Christ Jesus. Barth was clear that "the ministry of reconciliation also commits us to work honestly and earnestly for peace among the nations." Efforts for peacemaking should be supported in every way. Christians cannot withdraw into a cozy spirituality of personal faith. We must be involved fully in the world, including with the world's most urgent problems—especially when it concerns working for peace.

Before his death in 1968, Barth recognized the threat nuclear weapons pose to the peace of the planet. Their use cannot be sanctioned. Barth wrote that "in view of the means of mass destruction war is less than ever a possible solution of political and ideological

46. Barth, *Fragments Grave and Gay*, 58.

tension between nations and power blocs." Conflicts between peoples cannot be allowed to escalate toward use of ultimate weapons. Work for peace!

78

The Demands for Justice

> It is true that one cannot deduce orders of justice valid for all ages from God's righteousness. Yet that righteousness demands that all earthly justice respect the dignity of man created and redeemed by God, uphold the equality of all before the law, assure the protection of the weak, and allow room for the proclamation of the gospel and the life of love for one's neighbor.[47]

++++

When he thought about God's justice and what it means for the church and the world, Barth recognized that "one cannot deduce orders of justice valid for all ages from God's righteousness." No structures or organized configurations of justice are inviolable and valid for all times and places. Cultures and societies, and their needs, vary.

But Barth did believe God's righteous demanded key theological convictions. Primary is that earthly justice must uphold human dignity. Humans created in the image of God and redeemed by Jesus Christ are to be respected, and their basic humanity honored. All persons should be equal under the laws of a nation, without preferential treatment given or discrimination practiced. Justice under the law should protect the weak. Those without resources or power should be cared for in just and equitable ways, their rights protected. Justice, under God, also demands room in society for "the proclamation of the gospel and the life of love for one's neighbor." The freedom of the gospel should be a dimension of societal life, so the commands of God can be lived out in the church's witness and ministries.

47. Barth, *Fragments Grave and Gay*, 57.

Human justice is to reflect God's justice in its concern for the weak and powerless, its emphasis on equity and equality; and its promotion of human freedom, so all may experience the true freedom God gives in Jesus Christ.

79

The Church's Concern for Justice

> The gospel of God's righteousness and the commandment to love one's neighbor commit the church to a concern for earthly justice. Such concern shows itself in the witnessing to God's commandments, in the demonstration of common humanity in earthly vocation, and in the willingness to suffer injustice rather than commit unjust deeds.[48]

++++

The church is theological at its core. It exists by God's grace and lives by God's grace. It seeks to follow God's commandments. God's commands to the church express God's righteousness, who God is. Foremost among these commands—as known in Jesus Christ—is the command to love our neighbor (Mark 12:31).

This command is given to each Christian and to the church as the whole body of Christ. The church expresses love on a corporate scale, in society, through its commitment and actions for justice. Barth put it clearly when he wrote that "the gospel of God's righteousness and the commandment to love one's neighbor commit the church to a concern for earthly justice." Love in action is working for justice for all persons, throughout the earth.

Barth mentioned three ways the church's concern for justice is expressed: "the witnessing to God's commandments, in the demonstration of common humanity in earthly vocation, and in the willingness to suffer injustice rather than commit unjust deeds." The church witnesses to God's will and purposes for the world, according to God's commandments. It joins with all persons in shared humanity, as servants of God; and the church is resolute in avoiding unjust deeds, even when it may have to suffer injustice.

48. Barth, *Fragments Grave and Gay*, 57.

The church's commitment to justice involves it in concrete, practical actions on behalf of those in need of help in facing unjust structures and practices in society. "Do justice" (Mic 6:8)!

80

Every Meal Promises the Eternal Banquet

> In the Bible each meal, whether it be modest or sumptuous, is something sacred, for it is the promise of an eternal banquet, of an everlasting feast. In the Bible bodily and temporal life is sacred because it is the promise of life immortal and eternal.[49]

++++

In a fast-food world, we often eat on the run or rush through meals to get on to the next important thing we have to do. To take time and linger over a meal may be a luxury, or at least often not our standard practice.

What is most important, regardless of what we eat or drink or what the source of food may be, is that we recognize the theological importance of our meals. We eat and drink because of the grace of God in providing for our human needs. So, it is no wonder we say a prayer or blessing before a meal!

But also, each meal, as Barth points out, "whether it be modest or sumptuous, is something sacred, for it is the promise of an eternal banquet, of an everlasting feast." In the Lord's Supper, we anticipate the coming of Jesus and the eternal, messianic banquet of the saints in glory (Luke 13:29). The supper is the model for all our meals. Each meal, in which God provides for our needs now, also looks to the future in anticipation of the great eternal banquet in the kingdom of God. Our "bodily and temporal" lives are sacred since they too promise our "life immortal and eternal." Our meals sustain our lives and anticipate the glorious, eternal banquet which is an "everlasting feast."

49. Barth, *Prayer*, 49.

Let's keep an eternal perspective when we participate in a meal. In each meal we are eating and drinking with Jesus. Every meal promises the eternal banquet. Each meal presents God's grace to us, now and forever!

81

Anticipating the Eschaton

> We are guests at his table and so no longer separated from himself. Thus in this sign the witness of his meal is united to the witness of the Holy Spirit. It tells us really, you shall not die but live, and proclaim the Lord's works! *You*! . . . Since we receive the testimony of the Lord's Supper, we already live here and now in anticipation of the eschaton, when God will be all in all.[50]

++++

There are many meanings to the Lord's Supper. In the supper, we look back to the death of Jesus Christ as we receive the bread and wine, Christ's body and blood. In the supper, we realize by faith that Jesus is present with us in the church community and in our own lives. We also anticipate the future as we proclaim the Lord's death "until he comes" (1 Cor 11:23–26).

Barth believed the Lord's Supper should be a joyous meal, not a meal of mourning, but joyful because we are celebrating eternal life in the midst of our lives here and now. Jesus Christ is with us. As Barth wrote: "We are guests at his table and so no longer separated from himself. Thus in this sign the witness of his meal is united to the witness of the Holy Spirit."

Even more, Barth said, "It tells us really, you shall not die but live, and proclaim the Lord's works! *You*!" This is the great message of faith and hope for each of us. We live and proclaim! God uses *us!*

In the supper, "we already live here and now in anticipation of the eschaton, when God will be all in all" (1 Cor 15:58). This is our future destiny to dream about: God's eternal future includes us forever! Here and now we celebrate this joyous meal in hope and expectancy of the eternal reign of God!

50. Barth, *Dogmatics in Outline*, 155.

82

In Death Is Our Gracious God

> We can only cling to the fact, but we can really do so, that even in our death and as its Lord he will be our gracious God, the God who is for us, and that this is the ineffable sum of all goodness, so that everything that happens to us in death will in some way necessarily work together for good.[51]

++++

We live on this earth according to the days given by God. Our life has a beginning and an end. The physical resources of all persons will be exhausted, in some way. We live. We die.

What happens beyond death is not known in the same way other experiences are known. Death is the great mystery, the great unknown.

Barth asserts that at our "ending time,"[52] the God who awaits us in death is the God we know as the Lord of death. This is the "gracious God" we know as the one who is for us (for man). We know this gracious God as for us in Jesus Christ. Death is under the sign of God's judgment. But this judgment has taken place in the death of Jesus Christ for the sin of the world.

Thus, wrote Barth, "we can only cling to the fact, but we can really do so, that even in our death and as its Lord he will be our gracious God, the God who is for us, and that this is the ineffable sum of all goodness, so that everything that happens to us in death will in some way necessarily work together for good" (see Rom 8:28).

The God we know in life is the God we also know in death. This God gives us the greatest good we can imagine and need: God is "for us" (Rom 5:8; 8:31). Death awaits. Awaiting also is the gracious God!

51. Barth, *Church Dogmatics* III/2, 610.

52. "Ending Time" is Barth's title for the final portion of the section "Man in His Time," in *Church Dogmatics* III/2, 587–640.

83

Don't Lose Hope!

But keep your chin up! Never mind! "He will reign!"[53]

++++

The night before Karl Barth died, he spoke by phone with Eduard Thurneysen, his friend of sixty years. Barth died the following night, on December 10, 1968. As his biographer and assistant, Eberhard Busch, recounts it: "He died peacefully some time in the middle of the night. He lay there as though asleep, with his hands gently folded from his evening prayers. So his wife found him the next morning, while in the background a record was playing the Mozart with which she had wanted to waken him."[54]

Thurneysen and Barth discussed the current gloomy world situation. Then, Thurneysen recalled Barth had said, "But keep your chin up! Never mind! 'He will reign!'"—quoting a saying of Christoph Blumhardt.

At the end, in the midst of the depressing world situation all around, Barth's word was: "Don't lose hope!" Continue to have faith and trust God. God's kingdom is coming. We can wait for it. But God's kingdom is sure. God will reign!

Barth's hope, expressed in his last conversation, is the word for us as well. We have plenty of reasons to think the world is dark and depressing. Within itself, the world gives us no cause for optimism. But in the face of it all is Christian hope, grounded in God's word in Jesus Christ: God will reign! Christ will reign! As the angel promised Mary about Mary's son, our Lord Jesus:,"of his kingdom there will be no end" (Luke 1:33).

Barth's faith was grounded in Jesus Christ. So is ours. For, "through him you have come to trust in God, who raised him from

53. Busch, *Karl Barth*, 498.

54. See Busch, *Karl Barth*, 498.

the dead and gave him glory, so that your faith and hope are set on God" (1 Pet 1:21).

84

A Relative of the Donkey

> If I have done anything in this life of mine, I have done it as a relative of the donkey that went its way carrying an important burden.[55]

++++

When Karl Barth turned eighty years of age, his friends gathered and Barth gave a speech. He spoke about his life and what he had hoped to be and do as a theologian and a Christian.

One image stood out. Barth referenced the donkey that "was permitted" to carry Jesus into Jerusalem on Palm Sunday (Matt 21:1–11). Barth said: "If I have done anything in this life of mine, I have done it as a relative of the donkey that went its way carrying an important burden."

Jesus' disciples told the donkey's owner that the Lord needed the donkey. Barth continued to say that "and so it seems to have pleased God to have used me at this time, just as I was."

This image of humbleness and obedience relates to us all. Are we willing to be "a relative to the donkey," to be used by God when and where we are needed? Many would prefer to be celebrities, grab attention for what they do, even in the name of Jesus. The cult of personality affects the Christian community. The spotlight must be turned on us.

But in humility, as disciples of Jesus, we do even the smallest things for his sake. We are a witness—not to ourselves, but to our Lord. We give "a cup of cold water" (Matt 10:42) knowing it is the little things that are big in the heart of God.

55. Barth, "Karl Barth's Speech on the Occasion of his Eightieth Birthday Celebrations," *Fragments Grave and Gay*, 116.

We give ourselves to be used by Jesus, in most humble roles, seeking not self-glory, but the glory of the Word who "became flesh and lived among us" (John 1:14), Jesus Christ!

Sources Quoted

Note that in this devotional volume the use of capital letters in quotations has been conformed to contemporary conventions in order to make reading the book smoother. For similar reasons spellings have been Americanized.

Barth, Karl. *Call for God: New Sermons from Basel Prison.* Translated by A. T. Mackay. London: SCM, 1967.

———. *The Christian Life: Church Dogmatics IV/4, Lecture Fragments.* Translated by Geoffrey W. Bromiley. Grand Rapids: Eerdmans, 1981.

———. *Christmas.* Translated by Bernhard Citron. Edinburgh: Oliver and Boyd, 1959.

———. *Church Dogmatics.* Translated by T.F. Torrance et al., and edited by Geoffrey W. Bromiley et al. 13 vols. Edinburgh: T. & T. Clark, 1956–75. (German edition: *Die kirchliche Dogmatik.* 1932–67).

———. *Credo.* New York: Scribner's Sons, 1962.

———. *Deliverance to the Captives.* Translated by Marguerite Wieser. 1959. Reprint. New York: Harper & Row, 1978.

———. *Dogmatics in Outline.* Translated by G. T. Thomson. 1949. Reprint. New York: Harper & Row, 1959.

———. *The Epistle to the Ephesians.* Introductory essays by Francis Watson and John Webster. Edited by R. David Nelson. Translated by Ross M. Wright. Grand Rapids: Baker Academic, 2017.

———. *Epistle to the Philippians: 40th Anniversary Edition.* Introductory essays by Bruce L. McCormack and Francis B. Watson. Translated by James W. Leitch. Louisville: Westminster John Knox, 2002.

———. *The Epistle to the Romans.* Translated by Edwyn C. Hoskyns. New York: Oxford University Press, 1968.

———. *Ethics.* Edited by Dietrich Braun. Translated by Geoffrey W. Bromiley. New York: Seabury, 1981.

———. *Evangelical Theology: An Introduction.* Translated by Grover Foley. 1963. Reprint. London: Collins, 1969.

———. *Fragments Grave and Gay*. Edited by Martin Rumscheidt. Translated by Eric Mosbacher. London: Collins, 1971.

———. *God Here and Now*. Translated by Paul M. van Buren. 1964. Reprint. London: Routledge, 2003.

———. *God in Action*. Translated by E. G. Homighausen and Karl J. Ernst. Manhasset, NY: Round Table, 1963.

———. *The Heidelberg Catechism for Today*. Translated by Shirley C. Guthrie Jr. Richmond, VA: John Knox, 1963.

———. *The Humanity of God*. Richmond, VA: John Knox, 1963.

———. *The Knowledge of God and The Service of God According to the Teaching of the Reformation*. The Gifford Lectures Delivered in the University of Aberdeen in 1937 and 1938. Translated by J. L. M. Haire and Ian Henderson. New York: Scribner's Sons, 1939.

———. *Prayer: 50th Anniversary Edition*. Edited by Don E. Saliers from the translation of Sara F. Terrien, with essays by I. John Hesselink et al. Louisville: Westminster John Knox, 2002.

———. *The Word of God and Theology*. Translated by Amy Marga. London: T. & T. Clark, 2011.

———. *The Word of God and the Word of Man*. Translated by Douglas Horton. New York: Harper & Row, 1957.

Busch, Eberhard. *Karl Barth: His Life from Letters and Autobiographical Texts*. Translated by John Bowden. 1976. Reprint. Eugene, OR: Wipf & Stock, 2005.

Luther, Martin. *Luther's Works*. Philadelphia: Fortress, 1959.

———. *Luther's Works*. St. Louis: Concordia, 1972.

McConnachie, John. "The Teaching of Karl Barth: A New Positive Movement in German Theology." *The Hibbert Journal* 25 (April 1927) 385–400.

Selected Resources for Further Reflection

Barth, Karl. *A Unique Time of God: Karl Barth's WWI Sermons*. Translated and edited by William Klempa. Louisville: Westminster John Knox, 2016.

Barth, Karl, and William H. Willimon. *The Early Preaching of Karl Barth: Fourteen Sermons with Commentary by William H. Willimon*. Translated by John E. Wilson. Louisville: Westminster John Knox, 2009.

Bender, Kimlyn J. *Karl Barth's Christological Ecclesiology*. Eugene, OR: Cascade, 2013.

Bloesch, Donald G. *Jesus Is Victor! Karl Barth's Doctrine of Salvation*. Nashville: Abingdon, 1976.

Bromiley, Geoffrey W. *Introduction to the Theology of Karl Barth*. Grand Rapids: Eerdmans, 1979.

Burnett, Richard, ed. *The Westminster Handbook to Karl Barth*. The Westminster Handbooks to Christian Theology. Louisville: Westminster John Knox, 2013.

Busch, Eberhard. *The Great Passion: An Introduction to Karl Barth's Theology*. Edited and annotated by Darrell L. and Judith J. Guder. Translated by Geoffrey W. Bromiley. Grand Rapids: Eerdmans, 2004.

Cocksworth, Ashley. *Karl Barth on Prayer*. T. & T. Clark Studies in Systematic Theology. London: Bloomsbury T. & T. Clark, 2015.

Franke, John R. *Barth for Armchair Theologians*. Illustrations by Ron Hill. Louisville: Westminster John Knox, 2006.

Harnack, Adolf. *What Is Christianity?* Translated by Thomas Bailey Saunders. New York: Putnam's Sons, 1901.

Hunsinger, George. *How to Read Karl Barth: The Shape of His Theology*. New York: Oxford University Press, 1991.

Mangina, Joseph L. *Karl Barth: Theologian of Christian Witness*. Louisville: Westminster John Knox, 2004.

McKim, Donald K. *Coffee with Calvin: Daily Devotions*. Louisville: Westminster John Knox, 2013.

———. *Ever a Vision: A Brief History of Pittsburgh Theological Seminary, 1959–2009*. Grand Rapids: Eerdmans, 2009.

———. *Moments with Martin Luther: 95 Daily Devotions.* Louisville: Westminster John Knox, 2016.

———. *Mornings with Bonhoeffer: 100 Reflections on the Christian Life.* Nashville: Abingdon, 2018.

———, ed. *How Karl Barth Changed My Mind.* 1986. Reprint. Eugene, OR: Wipf & Stock, 1998.

McKim, Donald K., and Roger R. Keller. "A Dialogue on the Theology of Karl Barth." In *Mormonism in Dialogue with Contemporary Christian Theologies*, edited by Donald W. Musser and David L. Paulsen, 19–66. Macon, GA: Mercer University Press, 2007.

O'Collins, Gerald. *Jesus: A Portrait.* Luton: Andrews UK, 2010.

Olson, Roger. "Did Karl Barth Really Say 'Jesus Loves Me, This I Know...?" *Patheos* (blog), January 24, 2013. https://www.patheos.com/blogs/rogereolson/2013/01/did-karl-barth-really-say-jesus-loves-me-this-i-know/.

Rogers, Jack, and Donald K. McKim. *The Authority and Interpretation of the Bible.* 1979. Reprint. Eugene, OR: Wipf & Stock, 1999.

Sanders, Fred. "The Kingdom in Person." http://scriptoriumdaily.com/the-kingdom-in-person/.

Webster, John. *Barth's Ethics of Reconciliation.* Cambridge: Cambridge University Press, 1995.

———, ed. *The Cambridge Companion to Karl Barth.* Cambridge: Cambridge University Press, 2000.